A Gospel Trilogy

by
W. Cleon Skousen

Second Printing May 2011
Third Printing May 2020
Fourth Printing January 2025

Published by
Ensign Publishing Co.
Salt Lake City, Utah
www.skousen2000.com
hdskousen@gmail.com

The Building Blocks
of the Universe

This talk was first presented, at the invitation of L.D.S. Mission President Mike Glauser, to approximately 180 missionaries at the Georgia Atlanta Mission on November 2-3, 2000.

Introduction

One of the most gratifying things about going on a mission is the opportunity to really learn about the gospel. And we learn it on two levels.

The first level is what Paul calls the MILK level of the gospel – learning WHAT the actual requirements of the gospel are to lead us back to the presence of the Father; for example, faith, repentance, baptism, the gift of the Holy Ghost, obeying the commandments and enduring to the end. Of course, we don't minimize the sacred importance of the MILK level because it tells you in the most simple terms WHAT you must do to reach the celestial kingdom.

The second level is what Paul called the MEAT level which explains WHY each principle of the gospel is essential and HOW it works. So the milk is the WHAT of the gospel. The meat is the WHY and the HOW. The difference between milk and meat is made very clear in the scriptures. Here is how Paul distinguished between these two different levels of gospel study. He said:

> *"I have fed you with milk and not with meat; for hitherto ye were not able to bear it, neither yet now are ye able." (1 Corinthians 3:2)*

> *"Ye have need that one teach you again which be*

the first principles of the oracles of God; and are become such as have need of milk, and not of strong meat. For every one that useth milk is unskillful in the word of righteousness; for he is a babe. But strong meat belongeth to them that are of full age, even those who by reason of [habitual] use have their senses exercised to discern both good and evil. Therefore ["NOT" according to Joseph Smith] leaving the principles of the doctrine of Christ, LET US GO ON UNTO PERFECTION; not [repeatedly] laying again the foundation of repentance from dead works, and of faith toward God." (Hebrews 5:12-14 plus 6:1)

Isaiah says the meat belongs to those "who understand doctrine and are weaned from the milk. . . For precept must be upon precept, line upon line." (Isaiah 28:9-10)

Of course the great challenge to Joseph Smith as the prophetic head of this new dispensation was the fact that he did not receive new knowledge merely line upon line and precept upon precept but LAYER upon LAYER. Sometimes these layers were so enriched with heavy doctrines of gospel meat that Joseph's associates choked on them and denounced both Joseph and the most recent layer of revelation as false and unacceptable. But Joseph's time was short. He could not wait for those who lagged behind. Consequently, ten members of the original Quorum of the Twelve faltered. The two apostles who stood valiantly with the prophet were Brigham Young and Heber C. Kimball.

While on a mission we concentrate on teaching the milk because these are the plain and simple things that are essential to get us back to the Father's Celestial Kingdom. They tell us WHAT to do. The key to success on the milk level is OBEDIENCE, a willingness to follow the essential requirements of the Gospel. Notice that Paul became upset with the saints in his day because he couldn't get them to go beyond the milk and learn the gospel meat AND THEREBY GO ON UNTO PERFECTION. Notice Isaiah's warning that the meat of the gospel cannot be digested by swallowing it in gulps. It must be prayerfully pondered, precept upon precept and line upon line.

The Blessing of Having a Great Teacher

I got into the meat of the gospel shortly after I arrived in the British Mission. I was only 17 when I was called on a mission and upon arriving in England I found out that Elder John A. Widtsoe was presiding over all the missions in Europe and he had his headquarters in England. That meant that once in awhile I would get to see him.

President Widtsoe was an apostle and a member of the Council of the Twelve. He had been the president of two universities, was a famous scientist, and a member of the Royal Society of England. By reputation he was considered to be one of the foremost scholars of the gospel in the entire church and had written books on the teachings of both Joseph Smith and the Discourses of Brigham Young.

One day when we were on the train together, I was bold enough to ask Elder Widtsoe a gospel question. I didn't realize it at the time, but my question turned out to be the most profound question in the entire gospel.

I said, "Elder Widtsoe, Why did Jesus have to be crucified?"

He paused and then said, "Who told you to ask me that question?"

I said, "Well nobody. It's my question. When I was a small boy in Canada they would tell us at Easter time how Jesus was lacerated with a whip, how he had a crown of thorns put on his head, with blood running down his face, and how he was nailed to the cross and suffered the most terrible agony. I wondered who in the world wanted all that suffering? If it had a purpose, what was it? Furthermore, how did the crucifixion of Jesus have anything to do with my salvation?"

Elder Widtsoe thought for a moment and then he said: "I could answer your questions, but you wouldn't understand the answers. You don't know enough about your Heavenly Father."

So I said, "Would you teach me?"

It was an audacious thing to ask a heavily burdened General Authority, but after a moment he said, "Since it is your question, maybe you would have enough curiosity and tenacity to pursue the rather tedious task of learning about it – line upon line and precept upon precept – that is the only way you can get the whole picture."

So that's how I stumbled into one of the greatest blessings of my entire life. I became a student of the meat of the gospel under the guidance of Apostle John A. Widtsoe.

— Part 1 —

Everything in Existence is Made Out of Just Two Things

A Surprise Beginning

Elder Widtsoe started me out about a hundred miles away from my original question concerning the crucifixion.

He asked me if I knew that everything in existence was made out of just two things. Well, I had just graduated from high school and I had learned in chemistry about elements. I told him there weren't just two. Chemists had identified over a hundred different elements.

"Oh," he said, "each element is made up of millions of these two tiny particles that I am talking about." So I asked him what these two tiny particles were.

He said: "When the prophet Lehi was on his death bed, he explained to his sons that everything in existence is made out of these two tiny building blocks. See if you can find what he called them in the book of 2 Nephi."

I asked him why he didn't give me the chapter and verse. He said, "Oh, I wouldn't deprive you of the thrill of finding them." This was characteristic of my entire training under John A. Widtsoe. He would describe the principle and tell me ABOUT where to find it and then leave it up to me. I finally located Lehi's statement. He said:

> *"There is a God, and he hath created ALL things, both the heavens and the earth, and all things that in them are, BOTH THINGS TO ACT AND THINGS TO BE ACTED UPON."* (2 Nephi 2:14)

Elder Widtsoe then said, "Heavenly Father has called the thing which *acts* by a certain name and the thing which is *acted upon* by another name. These are the two building blocks out of which the Lord has made everything in the entire universe. See if you can find out what he calls them. You will find these names about three-fourths of the way through the Doctrine and Covenants."

I really had to dig for those verses. Finally I found the names of these building blocks in section 93, verses 29-33.

The Lord said that the thing which "acts" is called an "intelligence" and that which is "acted upon" is called "element" or primal matter. He said these building blocks always existed. They are eternal. (D&C 93:29, 33) They cannot be created and they cannot be destroyed, but they can be organized, DIS-organized and RE-organized.

Since the intelligence is the ingredient that "acts," it is assumed that the elements are inert, or as some have said, "It is just "stuff." However, Brigham Young said that these tiny bits of primal matter or inert particles of stuff, are "capacitated to receive Intelligence." (Journal of Discourses, 7:2) In fact, Brigham Young – who was tutored by the prophet Joseph Smith – seems to have had a complete grasp of the nature of intelligence and its association with primal matter. He said:

> *"There is an eternity of matter, and it is all acted upon and filled with a portion of divinity. [God's organized intelligences] Matter is to exist; it cannot be annihilated. Eternity is without bounds and is filled with matter; and there is no such thing as empty space. And matter is capacitated to receive intelligence . . . matter can be organized and brought forth into intelligence, and to possess more intelligence, and to continue to increase in intelligence . . . learn those principles that organized matter [can be made] into animals, vegetables, and into intelligent beings capacitated to receive intelligence."*
> (Brigham Young, *Journal of Discourses*, vol. 7, p. 2-3)

Is There Intelligence in Everything?

These principles were thoroughly understood by Joseph Smith and the early brethren. As Apostle John A. Widtsoe said:

> *"It was clearly comprehended by the Prophet [Joseph Smith] and his associates that intelligence is the vivifying force of all creation – animate or inanimate – the rock and tree and beast and man, have ascending degrees of intelligence."* (John A. Widtsoe, *Joseph Smith, Seeker After Truth*, Deseret News Press, pp. 150- 151)

And as Brigham Young said:

> *"There is life [or intelligence] in all matter throughout the vast extent of all the eternities; it is in the rock, the sand, in water, air, the gases, and, in short, in every description and organization of matter, whether it be solid, liquid, or gaseous, particle operating with particle."* (*Journal of Discourses*, vol. 3, p. 277)

How the Father Manages His Vast Host of Intelligences

These intelligences have each attached themselves to particles of matter. After this has occurred Abraham refers to them as "organized intelligences." (Abraham 3:22) God can talk to these intelligences and after they have been thoroughly trained they can conform to the highly complex instruction they receive from the Father, the Son, or members of the Priesthood authorized to perform certain acts under the guidance of the Father or the Son.

The Lord says this elaborate process of training this host of eternal entities to conform to the elaborate complexity of God's design is by having "intelligence cleave unto intelligence" according to a prescribed pattern. (D&C 88:40) Scientists are gradually identifying these complex patterns and have mapped out their intricate composition. The patterns are unique for each entity throughout nature and are referred to as their DNA.

— Part 2 —

How Do I Get Acquainted With My Own Individual Intelligence?

I asked Elder Widtsoe what an "intelligence" would look like. He told me to look in the mirror since I was an intelligence. I said, "You mean all of me?" He said, "No, just the little 'I Am' in you that Heavenly Father has been training ever since he brought you in from outer darkness."

He continued, "We know you were valiant during your training as an intelligence because Father gave you a spirit body patterned after his own. And because you were valiant in the spirit world he has allowed you to have a physical body with millions of intelligences organized in your temporal tabernacle and faithfully serving you here on earth."

"Well," I asked, "where IS my personal intelligence?"

He said, "Put your hand on top of your head. Is that above you or below you?" I said, "It's above me."

He said, "Take hold of your chin. Is that above you or below you?" I replied, "That's below me."

"Take hold of your ear." I said, "That's beside me."

Then Elder Widtsoe asked, "Where is this little ME you keep talking about?"

I said, "It must be way back in there somewhere."

He replied, "I think so."

I asked, "Is my hand part of ME?" He said, "No. That hand is YOURS, but it is not the ME or little I AM you keep talking about."

I asked Elder Widtsoe why we call the ME which is in each of us, "a little I AM."

He said, "Close your eyes. Now tell me if you think you actually exist. It is interesting that you actually KNOW you exist. As the famous philosopher, Rene Descartes, declared: 'Cogito, ergo sum – I think, therefore I am.' Descartes was a Frenchman who lived from 1596 to 1650 and is considered by many to be the father of modern philosophy. He believed everything consisted of two things: thinking substance – the mind – and extended substance – or matter. One thing he knew for certain, the fact that he personally existed. And by carefully following a series of propositions, he was certain that God also existed."

At this point, Elder Widtsoe said: "Now, with your eyes shut, first notice your self awareness and then notice that everything else exists OUTSIDE of you. It is outside of your self-existing entity. Like Descartes you know that YOU ARE, or to make it more personal you can say, I AM. This is your individual intelligence talking. You not only know you exist but God says you ALWAYS existed. You didn't have to be created because you were always there. And God was always there. He wasn't always God but he was always an existing entity. When Moses asked God what his name was, he said: 'I AM, that I AM.' (Exodus 3:14) In other words he has always been a self-existing being and we now know that he ascended under his Father's guidance until he became a God. Now, Elder Skousen, your little 'I AM' is on that same course of eternal progression. If you are faithful, you can become like your Heavenly Father."

A Further Examination of Where We Came From

I asked Elder Widtsoe: "If we always existed, where did we come from?" He said, "Outer Darkness." I asked, "How do we know that?"

He said, "The Lord has revealed what happens to the sons of perdition, and by tracking their disintegration we learn where WE came from. For example, Father Lehi was on his death bed when he addressed his two wicked sons, Laman and Lemuel. He said they were in danger of becoming sons of perdition. They had seen an angel and heard the voice of God reprimanding them for several hours. Lehi therefore said that if they continued to try to murder Nephi and refused to repent of their heinous sins, they would become sons of perdition. Then he told them what that meant. He said they would be stripped of their resurrected bodies, 'BOTH BODY AND SOUL.'" (2 Nephi 1:22)

Brigham Young describes the process of depriving sons of perdition of both body and soul as mentioned by Father Lehi. He said:

> *"They will be decomposed, both soul and body, and return to their native element. [In other words, the elements of their resurrected bodies will be united with the resurrected earth]. . . . They will be disorganized, and [it] will be as though they never had been, while WE will live and retain our identity, and contend against those principles which tend to death or dissolution. . . . I want to preserve my identity, so that you can see Brigham in the eternal worlds just as you see him now." (Journal of Discourses, vol 7:57)*

He further explained that Satan and his angels would be stripped of their spirits. In both cases this leaves the individual intelligence without any embodiment whatever. Each one has lost his former identity, with nothing remaining but the naked, individual intelligence.

No doubt this is what the Lord meant when he said:

> *"Whosoever repenteth not is HEWN down and cast into the fire; and there cometh upon them again a spiritual death, yea, a second death, for they are cut off again as to things pertaining to righteousness." (Helaman 14:18)*

And again:

> *"By and by the end cometh, and they are HEWN down and cast into the fire [of outer darkness], from whence there is no return." (3 Nephi 27:11)*

At that point I couldn't help asking "What happens to these stripped, disembodied, naked intelligences?"

Elder Widtsoe then called my attention to *Doctrine and Covenants*, 88:32 where it says that these afflicted entities will "RETURN AGAIN to their own place." The scripture says this means:

> *"They shall go away into outer darkness, where there is weeping, and wailing, and gnashing of teeth."* (D&C 133:73)

From all of this we learn that the scriptures clearly teach that we all originally came from outer darkness and the sons of perdition return AGAIN to the place from which we all originated.

Satan's Battle to Prevent the Disorganization of his Spirit Body

At the end of the Millennium the scripture says Satan will wage a ferocious war to prevent the disorganizing of his spirit body as described by Brigham Young. His war will also be to prevent the disorganizing of his followers including the resurrected sons of perdition.

The scripture says:

> *"And when the thousand years are expired, Satan shall be loosed out of his prison, and shall go out to deceive the nations which are in the four quarters of the earth, Gog and Magog, to gather them together to battle: the number of whom is as the sand of the sea. And they went up on the breadth of the earth, and compassed the camp of the saints about, and the beloved city, and fire came down from God out of heaven, and devoured them."*
> (Revelation 20: 7-9)

This was the destruction Satan and his hosts are determined to prevent. But they will lose the war. Then they will be "hewn" down. Satan and the third of the Father's children who followed after him will lose their spirit bodies whereas Cain, Judas Iscariot and all of the sons of perdition (who were on the Savior's side in the war in heaven and therefore qualified to get mortal bodies) lose their resurrected bodies because they betrayed God and were therefore resurrected without any glory or capacity to continue existing. (D&C 88:24) They are therefore "hewn" down with nothing left but the naked, disembodied intelligence. So what happens to these stripped, naked intelligences? We have already mentioned the scripture which describes their doom:

> *"These shall go away into outer darkness, where there is weeping and wailing and gnashing of teeth."* (D&C 133:73)

And in another place it says:

> *"And the devil that deceived them was cast into the lake of fire and brimstone, where the beast [Satan] and the false prophet are, and shall be tormented day and night FOR EVER AND EVER."* (Revelation 20:10)

Of course it would not be just for God to cast the bodies of the sons of perdition into outer darkness just because the master intelligence in charge of each spirit or resurrected sons of perdition had committed an unpardonable sin. Those tiny intelligences in those bodies had been obedient to God. Therefore, the material in the spirits and the resurrected bodies of Satan's hosts will be consigned back to the earth and thereafter be glorified when the earth is celestialized.

The great tragedy of all this is that all those who became servants of Satan can never return. (D&C 29:29) They cannot be swept up in some future round of creation and recycled. Having betrayed God after being endowed with tremendous spiritual blessings they have lost their place in God's program of eternal progression forever. Hundreds of millions of other intelligences are awaiting their turn. Because the sons of perdition have betrayed God they have completely forfeited their eternal blessings.

Can God or His Servants
Rearrange the Building Blocks?

Finally, I said to Elder Widtsoe, "Since everything is made out of the two simple building blocks consisting of intelligence and bits of primal matter, are there any instances when God has transposed one thing into something entirely different?"

"Yes," Elder Widtsoe replied. "God has done this for his prophets so they could comprehend the extent of the Father's supreme power. For example we have the story of Moses set forth in Exodus, Chapters 3 and 4." Here is what happened:

When Moses was 80 years of age the Lord commissioned him to go down into Egypt and bring out the enslaved children of Israel.

Moses had left Egypt at the age of 40 under a death warrant for slaying a slave master. Therefore Moses was afraid to return to Egypt. The Lord assured Moses that he would go with him, but Moses was still afraid. Therefore, the Lord determined to demonstrate to his newly called prophet that having the power of God to go with him was a fantastic advantage.

To illustrate his power, God commanded Moses to cast his shepherd's staff onto the ground. When he did so, the staff turned from the fibers of wood in the staff to the cellular flesh of a snake. This greatly frightened Moses and he began to flee, but the Lord told him to pick up the serpent by the tail and when he did so, the cellular flesh of the snake turned back into the wooden fibers of his shepherd's staff.

The Lord then told Moses to put his hand into his bosom. Moses was about to learn something very remarkable about a human hand. To begin with, it is made of dirt, just ordinary common dirt. When the spirit leaves that hand it returns to dirt. But that dirt is saturated with intelligences. So the Lord said to those little entities, don't go back to dirt but simulate leprosy. They did so, and when Moses was told by the Lord to withdraw his hand from his bosom he was horrified to see it dripping with incurable leprosy. He must have wondered what God was doing to him?

The Lord then told Moses to put his hand back in his bosom which he gingerly did. Then the Lord commanded the leprous cells to become healthy flesh as they were before. The Lord then told Moses to take his hand from his bosom and when he saw that it was now beautiful pink flesh he was greatly relieved and gratified beyond expression.

The Lord promised Moses other miracles if they were needed – such as turning water into blood. (Exodus 4:9)

However, this was sufficient to demonstrate the power of God to communicate with the intelligences in matter and thereby change wood to flesh and, later on, produce water gushing out of solid rock. (Numbers 20:11) In the final analysis, everything is made of just two things and God can communicate with the vast host of intelligences to have them become whatever he wishes.

Where Are the Gods Building Their Kingdoms?

It was also in the early part of my mission that I ran across a statement of the Lord in Section 71 of the Doctrine and Covenants addressed to Joseph Smith and Sidney Rigdon. It said:

> *"...open your mouths in proclaiming my gospel, the things of the kingdom, expounding the MYSTER-IES OUT OF THE SCRIPTURES."* (D&C 71:1)

I told Elder Widtsoe that I didn't know of any mysteries in the scriptures. They seemed very plain to me. Of course this was a 17-year-old missionary speaking.

Elder Widtsoe knew this young missionary needed a lesson in humility.

He said, "Elder Skousen, turn to section 88 of the Doctrine and Covenants. There are many mysteries in that section of the scripture, and I want to have you explain one of them to me." He said, "For example, I want you to read verse 37 describing God's 'space.'"

"Oh," I said. "Space is easy to define. It's everything from here on out."

"Wrong," said Elder Widtsoe. "Read verse 37." It said:

"And there are many kingdoms; for there is no space in which there is no kingdom; and there is no kingdom in which there is no space, either a greater or a lesser kingdom."

A careful analysis of this verse tells us two things. First that "space" is a defined region out in the eternities where the family of the Gods are building their vast network of kingdoms, and second, they do not build any kingdoms outside of "space" or the sacred region under their exclusive control. This is the somewhat hidden meaning of the phrase: "There is no kingdom in which there is no space." Elder Widtsoe said this is one of the mysteries in the scriptures.

I asked Elder Widtsoe why God would call this passage a "mystery in the scriptures." Elder Widtsoe said, "Well, that passage contained a revelation defining 'space,' and even though you had read it many times you never understood it. Until today it was a mystery to you." I was beginning to get the idea.

What Is Outside of Space?

This led me to ask Elder Widtsoe, "Since space is the sacred workshop of the Gods, what is outside or beyond space?"

Elder Widtsoe said the Gods call the region beyond space "outer darkness." So I asked, "What exists in outer darkness?" He said: "Vast, unlimited quantities of UNorganized intelligences and UNorganized bits of primal matter. These are the two building blocks we have been talking about. It is from these vast resources in outer darkness that the Gods gather out the vital elements or building blocks to set up each new round of creation."

Finally I asked: "Who is in charge of outer darkness?" He replied, "No one. The primitive intelligences and bits of primal matter exist in total, disorganized chaos without any organizing power over them or any influence to guide them."

Some of the early brethren suggested the Holy Spirit might be hovering over this outer darkness. Here is Brigham Young's response:

> *"Brother [Orson} Hyde was [dwelling] upon this same theory once, and in conversation with Brother Joseph Smith advanced the idea [that the Holy Spirit might be hovering over the boundless eternities which he mistakenly called boundless space.]*
>
> *"Brigham Young continued, "that after [Orson had been] portraying his views upon that theory very carefully and minutely, he asked brother Joseph what he thought of it. He [Joseph] replied that it appeared very beautiful, and he did not know of but one serious objection to it." Brother Hyde asked, "What is that?" Joseph replied, "It is not true."* (*Journal of Discourses* 4:266)

This is what led the Lord to remind the prophet Isaiah that, "Before me there was no God formed [for you], neither shall there be after me." (Isaiah 43:10)

In other words, it is a great blessing to be gathered in from outer darkness by our Heavenly Father and be allowed to participate in a round of creation. God wanted Isaiah to also know that if he should betray God and become a son of perdition, there would never be an opportunity to have some other God gather him up and give him another chance.

To help demonstrate these enlightening scriptures concerning "space" and the organizing of kingdoms by the family of the Gods, we have tried to portray them schematically (along with the scriptural references). This full illustration is located on page 46.

The Pathway to Godhood

The Father revealed so many things to Joseph Smith about himself, that the prophet was reluctant to share much of it with the Church until three months before his assassination. It was at the April conference of the Church in 1844 that he gave a funeral sermon in honor of King Follette who had just passed away. Joseph felt inspired to use the spiritual environment of this sacred occasion to tell the saints some amazing things about our Heavenly Father. He said:

> *"God himself was once as we are now, and is an exalted man, and sits enthroned in yonder heavens!"* (*Teachings of Joseph Smith*, p. 345)

This statement has stupendous implications. It means that the Father went through the same pattern of eternal progression we are now experiencing. This meant that our Heavenly Father, or Elohim, has his own Heavenly Father who gathered him up from outer darkness and gave him the opportunity to participate in a round of creation. This launched our Heavenly Father on a pathway of eternal progression which eventually allowed him to become an exalted being. Joseph Smith said:

> *"The first principles [or individual intelligences] of man are self-existent with God. God himself, finding he was in the midst of intelligences* and glory, because he was more intelligent, saw proper to institute laws whereby the rest [of the intelligences] could have a privilege to advance like himself. The relationship we have with God places us in a situation to advance in knowledge. He has power to institute laws*

to instruct the weaker intelligences, that they may be exalted with himself, so that they might have one glory upon another, and all that knowledge, power, glory, and intelligence which is requisite in order to save them in the world of spirits."

**(The recorder originally put the word "spirits" in this place, but B. H. Roberts noted that it should have been "intelligences." See Teachings of Joseph Smith, p. 352 Note)*

This inspired statement contains the following essential elements:

1. Elohim, our Father, was once in outer darkness with us.

2. But he was gathered up by a Heavenly Father and progressed during a round of creation in his Father's domain.

3. After perfecting himself by obtaining both a spiritual and temporal body, he was resurrected and attained the highest degree of the celestial kingdom in his Father's domain.

4. In the plan of eternal progression, any of the sons of God who reach this stage are eligible to be given the powers of Godhood.

As Brigham Young explained:

"In the resurrection, men who have been faithful and diligent in all things in the flesh, have kept their first and second estates, and [are] worthy to be crowned Gods, even the sons of God, will be ORDAINED TO ORGANIZE MATTER." (*Journal of Discourses* vol. 15, p. 137)

5. Once Elohim had been given this power to organize matter, he came back to the edge of space and gathered up from outer darkness those of us who were to comprise our present round of creation. He also scooped up a sufficient quantity of primal matter with which our intelligences could be "organized."

So this tells me how we got where we are. Our Heavenly Father came back for us so we could participate in a round of creation and progress just as he has done.

Ever since I learned this exciting information, I have earnestly thanked my Heavenly Father repeatedly for including me in this present round of creation. And I have thanked him for including my wife and my children and the host of wonderful people I have come to know as my friends. What a blessing for all of us to be together in this great adventure of eternal progression.

What It Means to Achieve Godhood

Eventually, all of the priesthood holders – who attain exaltation and are ordained to organize matter – will do exactly what our Father has done before us. We will go out to the edge of space as Father did and gather up from outer darkness a host of intelligences, together with an appropriate amount of primal matter, so that we can begin our own round of creation.

Thus we will learn for ourselves what it is like to be a God.

Our first task will be to sort out these billions of intelligences and organize them with bits of primal matter. Then we will teach them to love us and obey us as we unite them with one another in a vast array of orderly combinations. We will then explain to them how we plan to organize a galaxy of our own. This will help expand the "space" of the Gods and add to the glory of those who went before us.

A very significant part of this stage of training will be to help these individual intelligences decide where they want to fit into this vast new order of things. One might think that they will all want to become Gods, but not so. Abraham tells us that as the intelligences are graded they will choose different levels of existence according to their desires. (Abraham 3:19-22; *Teachings of Joseph Smith*, p. 373)

Some want to be part of the planet which will eventually be resurrected. Some will be attracted to participation in the kingdoms of plant life. Others will desire to be part of the animal kingdom. And a smaller segment which constitute the foremost intelligences will aspire to have opportunities comparable to that of their Heavenly Father.

The most significant aspect of this epic of training and decision-making is the fact that once the decisions are made they will last through all eternity. Each intelligence will not only choose its role in the spirit world and in earth life but also in the eternities following the resurrection.

Nevertheless, each intelligence will have had the satisfaction of knowing that it made its own free choice and thereby fixed the course of its development forever.

When it comes time for the launching of the spirit creation, each intelligence will take its chosen place. Joseph Smith describes this remarkable transition as the intelligences move eagerly from mere theoretical anticipation to actual participation.

He says:

> *"The organization of the spiritual and heavenly worlds, and of spiritual and heavenly beings, was agreeable to the most perfect order and harmony: their limits and bounds were fixed IRREVOCABLY and VOLUNTARILY subscribed to in their heavenly estate by THEMSELVES, and were by our first parents subscribed to upon this earth."* (Church History vol. VI, p. 51)

This tells us that after the intelligences have chosen the eternal role which they desire to fulfill, the signal will be given, and they will all immediately take their places in the most perfect order and harmonious arrangement. Then every intelligence in God's elaborate structure for this round of creation will be ready to receive its spiritual embodiment. With this exciting and glorious commencement of the spirit creation, the First Estate will have begun.

What About Those Who Desire to Become Like Heavenly Father?

It may seem puzzling that all the intelligences do not aspire to become Gods. However, when we reflect on the statement of Abraham that the intelligences are graded according to their attributes it is understandable why the intelligences of lesser development would resist the responsibilities associated with the higher levels of existence. In fact, the genius of each round of creation is that there are opportunities for participation which extend from the most simple involvement to the extremely complex responsibilities of Godhood.

The scriptures make it clear that an exalted being who is a member of the Priesthood and has been ordained to Godhood will undoubtedly encounter at least three monumental crises that can jeopardize his role as a Heavenly Father and threaten to destroy his immediate round of creation.

Three Heavenly Crises

The first crisis will be a revolution during the spirit creation. This occurs when an over-ambitious leader decides to challenge the Father and put himself in complete control of the whole round of creation.

How could this happen?

It is the very nature of intelligent beings who have risen to a level which they consider to be equal or superior to their Heavenly Father, to suddenly aspire to take over and replace the very being who has helped them gain their high status of achievement. Obviously this passionate aspiration of an arrogant spirit constitutes a challenge to a Heavenly Father since he must deal with this explosive eagerness lest it subvert and completely shatter that particular round of creation.

Therefore this is a major crisis even among heavenly beings. The Father must defuse this ambitious usurper and, if necessary, suppress an outbreak of an angry conflict in heaven. Restoring peace will be the first threatening crisis facing a Heavenly Father.

The second crisis will occur during the second estate when the Father's chosen Redeemer falters in terror as he draws near to the agonies connected with the redemptive sacrifice. However since the Father knows the end from the beginning he realizes that eventually the Chosen One will overcome his terror and fulfill his great calling. Nevertheless there is a moment of supreme crisis as this round of creation hangs perilously in the balance.

The third crisis comes at the the end of the Millennium when Satan mobilizes his vast host of followers to make his final desperate attempt to overthrow the Father and his Redeemer Son. The intensity of the final war is magnified by Satan's realization that if he loses this war, he and his followers will be disembodied and cast back into outer darkness as stripped naked intelligences. To prevent this horrible judgment of losing their very identity, they will make this war the most violent upheaval in all human history.

Of course, a Supreme Being in charge of a round of creation will know the end from the beginning. He will know that each of these crises will be successfully resolved, but this knowledge will not make the solution any less violent or strenuous to endure until it is over.

Of course, all of us know that up to the present time, our Heavenly Father has already passed through the first two crises in this round of creation. It is part of our education in this life to know what happened.

It all began when Elohim, our Heavenly Father, selected the most advanced intelligence in our family of his children to be trained for the role of general manager over this round of creation. He became the first born of all of the Father's children, and our Father gave him the name of Jehovah.

The Training of Jehovah

It was a long and somewhat tedious task to prepare Jehovah for Godhood. Amazingly, Jehovah had to attain the status of Godhood – even in the spirit world – before he could become the Father's general manager of this round of creation.

John the Baptist recorded the following concerning the Savior's initial training. This was later revealed to Joseph Smith:

> *"I, John saw that he [Jehovah] received not of the fullness at the first, but received grace for grace... and thus he was called the Son of God, because he received not of the fullness at the first."* (D&C 93:12-14)

Since the restoration of the gospel, we have learned myriads of exciting details concerning the early stages of our present round of creation. These all took place on the celestial residence of our

Heavenly Father located near the huge planet Kolob which is close to the center of our galaxy. (Abraham 3:2- 3)

We think of this opening period – when the vast quantity of intelligences were being gathered in from outer darkness and trained – as the first stage of our existence as part the Father's kingdom.

The Spirit Creation

Now the Father populated his celestial planet with a vast quantity of children. Paul said these children were all the "offspring" of the Father (Acts 17:29) but Jehovah is given credit for assembling the highly refined spiritual matter from which their spirit bodies were made. Thus we read:

> *"Therefore, in the beginning the Word was, for he was the Word even the messenger of salvation. . . The worlds were made by him; MEN WERE MADE BY HIM."* (D&C 93:8-10)

The scripture is plain that Jehovah was the general manager of the entire spirit creation – planets, people, plants and animals. (Moses 2:32-33) His intimate relation with the hosts of intelligences throughout this round of creation made him beloved just as they loved the Father. As we shall see later, this was absolutely essential to qualify him for his role as the Redeemer.

The First Council in Heaven

Finally the Father was ready to transfer this mighty host of spirit children to their own planet where they could be trained and prepared for the Second Estate. This would be a tremendous undertaking and so the Father held a massive council meeting with all his children participating. The scripture says:

> *"Now the Lord had shown unto me, Abraham, the intelligences that were organized [with spirits] before the world was. . . And there stood one among them that was like unto God."*

Notice that this leader was not God, but someone "like unto God" who would undoubtedly be Jehovah or Jesus Christ. This person knew what the Father wanted done, and so he said:

> *"We will go down for there is space there, and we will take of these materials, and we will make an earth whereon these may dwell. And we will prove them herewith, to see if they will do all things whatsoever the Lord their God shall command them."* (Abraham 3:24-25)

The structuring of this new planet was a colossal undertaking. As Brigham Young taught, it was built in the vicinity of the Father's celestial residence which was near the planet Kolob. (Journal of Discourses vol. 17, p. 143)

The preparation of the earth took millions of years. It had to provide the resources for tens of thousands of generations of both animals and mankind.

In contemplation of this mighty task, the Lord said:

> *"Whom shall I send? And one answered like unto the Son of Man: Here am I send me. And another answered and said: Here am I send me. And the Lord said: I will send the first. And the second was angry, and kept not his first estate; and at that day many followed after him."* (Abraham 3:27-28)

Many may not have realized it, but the seeds had been sown for the war in heaven. But that would come much later.

The Work of the First Estate

Meanwhile there were divine labors that had to be performed by Jehovah and the council of the "noble and great ones" such as Abraham, Isaac, Jacob, Moses, Joseph Smith and others who would be the leaders of the various dispensations.

Tens of billions of the Father's children also had to be sorted out and designated for the various nations and empires that would occupy the earth during the seven thousand years of its temporal existence.

The work was further complicated by the fact that empires and the distribution of population had to be calculated in terms of the availability of the Lord's leaders, called Israel or Soldiers of God.

Moses describes this challenging task. He says:

". . .ask thy father, and he will shew thee; thy elders and they will tell thee, when the most high divided to the nations their inheritance, when he separated the sons of Adam, he set the bounds of the people ACCORDING TO THE NUMBER OF THE CHILDREN OF ISRAEL." (Deuteronomy 32:7-8)

Another arduous task during the preexistence was ordaining all of those who were designated for Priesthood leadership during the Second Estate. Priesthood is simply a "call to service," and many of those who were eligible for the Priesthood rejected this "call to service." Alma describes this phenomenon:

"And this is the manner after which they were ordained being called and prepared from the foundation of the world according to the foreknowledge of God, on account of their exceeding faith and good works. . .while others would reject the Spirit of God on account of the hardness of their hearts and blindness of their minds, while if it had not been for this THEY MIGHT HAVE HAD AS GREAT PRIVILEGE AS THEIR BRETHREN."
(Alma 13:3-4)

The War in Heaven

After the preparations for the Second Estate were in order the Father called another massive council of all his children. The purpose was to choose a Redeemer or mediator without which this entire round of creation would be lost.

First of all, the Father explained that with each round of creation there has to be a Redeemer. He then asked who would provide the redemptive sacrifice. Suddenly, a fantastic development occurred. Lucifer leaped forward.

Satan hated the idea of an atoning sacrifice which required an infinite quantity of suffering by the mediator which would be so compelling that the hosts of intelligences would overlook the sins of the repentent and grant all the special blessings for which the

Savior might plead in our behalf as we ascended the pathway of eternal progression.

It is highly significant that Satan had not kept his first estate (Abraham 4:28) but spent his time conjuring up a scheme which he wanted the Father to accept in place of the atoning sacrifice which the family of the Gods had used down through the eternities. Satan was so proud of his scheme that he wanted the full honor of inventing it. (D&C 29:36)

The core of Satan's plan was to suspend free agency during the Second Estate and force the Father's children to conform to celestial law so that none of them would be lost because of sin. He carefully explained how his marvelous scheme would operate. Under Satan's plan there would be:

- No necessity for an atoning sacrifice.
- No sin would be allowed.
- No evil would be permitted.
- No suffering would have to be endured.
- No judgment would be required.
- No punishment would be inflicted.
- No failures would occur.

The entire family of the Father would be automatically saved under Satan's plan.

Of course, Satan had missed one important fact. The whole purpose of the Second Estate was to help the Father's children distinguish between good and evil. Their exposure to evil and the consequences of its influence was needed to galvanize them against the temptations of evil throughout eternity. But obviously, Satan's plan would not do this. It would actually deprive them of the capacity to experience evil or even recognize it. In fact, under Satan's plan the Father's children would go through life in a Luciferian strait jacket and learn nothing.

Therefore, when Jehovah perceived how the abominable plan of Satan was shrewdly designed to rob the Father of his throne and deprive Jehovah of his divine mission, he stepped forward and volunteered to go through the agonies of the redemptive sacrifice and thereby save this whole round of creation.

Immediately, the Father accepted the offer of Jehovah and rejected the subversive plan of Satan. Suddenly there was an uproar in heaven.

A large portion of this vast multitude liked the plan proposed by Satan. After all, it guaranteed them salvation without any effort on their part. It made all the choices for them. It eliminated the awful necessity of a blood sacrifice and it offered them complete salvation on a silver platter. This multitude completely agreed with Satan and they were willing to wage war to have it adopted.

So the Father's first great crisis roared out across the face of the new planet. But this war was fought in a peculiar way. No weapons were used. John the Beloved says the furious encounter was fought with argument and contentious debate. John says the servants of God fought with their testimonies. (Revelation 12:11)

The line of argument probably went something like this: If they followed Satan they would never get temporal bodies, They would even lose their spirit bodies.

It is interesting that those who labored on behalf of the Savior were called "The Soldiers of God" or "Israel" even in the preexistence. They testified with the most earnest passion that the only hope for the Father's children was to accept the Father's decision and follow Jehovah.

The casualty rate in this war was very high. In a very real way it was a war to the death. One third of the Father's vast host of offspring gambled away their legacy in God's Kingdom because they wanted the Father to adopt Satan's plan. No amount of reason and patient testimony-bearing would persuade them. Finally the Father felt compelled to command Michael to force the host of mutinous rebels into exile – across the veil and into the temporal world.

There, for the next six thousand years, the war would continue, and at the end of the seventh thousand years Satan and his followers would face their ultimate doom.

The Secret Mission of Jesus Christ

The first estate involved the selection of the Father's general manager for the structuring of this entire round of creation. Then the Father had to select a redeemer for the second estate. Satan thought the redemptive sacrifice of the Redeemer was virtually stupid and he therefore offered a plan that had never been tried before. When the Father chose the traditional plan with Jehovah or Jesus as the Redeemer, it caused a war in heaven because so many of the Father's children preferred Satan's plan. Satan wanted to eliminate the need for a Redeemer and guarantee salvation for all of the Father's children whether they wanted it or not. The only drawback to Satan's plan was the fact that it was based on force, and that is why the Father rejected it. This resulted in a war in heaven and concluded with one-third of the Father's children being ejected from their heavenly home.

The second estate was filed with perils under the traditional plan because everyone was at liberty to use his or her free agency so they could learn the difference between good and evil.

Of course, everyone would be held accountable for their abuse of free agency and would be punished for their misdeeds to the uttermost farthing.

But what if a person learned the difference between good and evil and wanted to avoid the punishment for past offenses. Could this be achieved?

The Father said there was a way if you knew how it worked. It was called the *Atonement.*

I urgently begged Elder John A. Widtsoe, with whom I had become acquainted, to explain the Atonement so I could comprehend it.

He began by carefully teaching me everything we have covered in *Trilogy 1.*

Then I was extremely anxious to have him get to the subject of the Atonement but, as usual, he began the discussion about a hundred miles away from the subject. In fact, he began with several questions. The first one was, "Where do you think our Father got his power?"

I suggested that he probably got it from HIS Father.

Elder Widtsoe said, "No, that is not correct. All he got from his Father was the authority or the keys to build a new round of creation. His Father did not give him the power to do it."

He then asked me a second question. "What makes a great bishop?" I told him I thought it was his ordination. "No," he said, "a bishop merely gets his AUTHORITY from his ordination, but his POWER to be a great bishop comes from the same place that God gets his."

In total frustration I asked, "Well then, where does God get his power?"

He said, "Two passages in the scriptures will give you the key. They are both from the Doctrine and Covenants. In Section 29, verse 36, Satans demands from the Father, 'Give me thine HONOR which is thy POWER.' Then in Section 63, verse 50 it says 'I am from ABOVE, and my power lieth BENEATH.'"

Elder Widtsoe then asked me what exists below God that honors him and gives him power, or, for that matter, what is there below a Bishop that gives him honor and therefore his power?

After a moment I said, "Well, with God it is the vast host of intelligences below God that honor him and therefore obey him. That certainly gives him power. And I suppose you could say the same thing about a bishop who is honored and obeyed and therefore from them he derives his power."

"Exactly!" said Elder Widtsoe. "This is a Priesthood principle. God and his servants acquire their power from those over whom they preside."

He continued, "I think you also know what makes a great bishop. It is everybody in their places for the Sunday services. It is deacons ready to serve the sacrament and worthy priests to bless it. It is teachers well prepared and radiant with the Spirit. It is young priests who make themselves conversant with the gospel and are anxious to be called on missions; it is vigilant Relief Society visiting teachers who are quick to detect the needs of the sick and the poor; tithes and offerings are given generously. These are the things that make people say, 'My, what a great bishop!' Obviously, his power comes from the support of his ward and the honor which is demonstrated by the members of the ward responding enthusiastically to his guidance and leadership."

Then he continued: "It is the same way with God. The honor and obedience which he receives from his vast legion of intelligences is what gives him his power."

How God Could Lose His Power

Then he surprised me by saying: "Did you know our Heavenly Father could lose that power?"

Of course that was a new doctrine to me, so I said, "How would that be possible? God is all-powerful. At least that is what I was always taught."

He said. "This amazing doctrine that God could lose his power is found in Alma chapter 42. There it plainly teaches that God is the great arbiter of the universe and each intelligence is depending on him to be absolutely honest, absolutely just, absolutely fair, and absolutely unchangeable, otherwise he 'WOULD CEASE TO BE GOD.' (Alma 42:13, 22, 25; Mormon 9:19) This is why the scripture says, 'God cannot look upon sin with the least degree of allowance,' (Alma 45:16; D&C 1:31) or if he did, he would cease to be God. Or, in other words, GOD WOULD FALL!"

Then he quickly added, "But, of course, he isn't going to fall because he knows how to prevent it. However, he wants us to know that he COULD fall. The Father wants us to know that if he doesn't maintain the confidence and honor of the host of intelligences in this round of creation, they would cease to honor him, and then cease to obey him, and without his honor, he would cease to be God. This is the powerful message set forth in Alma, chapter 42 and Mormon 9:19."

Having set down these amazing and somewhat surprising principles, he continued by saying: "Now we are ready to learn why the Atonement of Jesus Christ was indispensable to the Father. He needed Jesus to do something of supreme importance which the Father could not do himself. If he tried to redeem his children after they had fallen, he would cease to be God!"

Why Was the Fall Necessary?

Once I recognized the dilemma of the Father in the second estate, I asked, "Why was the Fall necessary?"

Briefly, here is what he told me. On the pathway of eternal progression it is necessary during the Second Estate for mankind to learn the difference between good and evil. They must not only know the difference between the two but they must engrain into their very souls a determination to embrace the good and abhor the evil. They must reject the evil with an instinctive vehemence that will characterize their behavior in the family of the Gods forever. This is of paramount importance, particularly for those who are aspiring to become Gods.

Our Heavenly Father knew that we are incapable of encountering sin without partaking of some of it. It is inherent in our very nature that by attempting to learn about sin we cannot avoid some degree of contamination. Therefore, under celestial law, our encounter with sin automatically cuts us off from the presence of the Father. Paul stated emphatically that because of the Fall: "ALL HAVE SINNED AND COME SHORT OF THE GLORY OF GOD." (Romans 3:23)

This leaves the Father helpless insofar as recovering his fallen children is concerned. This is what led Nephi to say:

"No unclean thing can dwell with God; wherefore ye [who have sinned while learning about sin] are cast off forever." (1 Nephi 10:21)

So What is the Answer?

But, of course, if we have learned the difference between good and evil but cannot get back to the domain of our Heavenly Father so as to continue our eternal progression, the Father's plan to have us exalted and become Gods is defeated. Therefore, the family of the Gods had to adopt a device that would justify the Father in restoring us to his celestial realm and continue our eternal progression without jeopardizing his Godhood.

The object of the Atonement was to get the Intelligences to overlook our imperfections IN SPITE of our sins. The Protestant scholars believed that this was accomplished by having Jesus "pay for our sins" through his suffering and thereby balance the scales of justice. However, this theory involves a monumental problem and that is the fact that it isn't "just" to have one person pay for the sins of another. Amulek points this out in Alma 34:11-12.

Amulek also explains that the Atonement is not based on trying to balance the scales of justice, but it is based on MERCY WHICH WIPES OUT THE DEMANDS OF JUSTICE. (Alma 34:15)

It turned out that this was the genius of the Atonement.

How Does the Atonement Work?

There are three essential requirements in a divine Atonement to accomplish something which the Father could never do himself. First, there must be someone who is loved by all the hosts of intelligences. They must love this person as much as they love God himself. This was achieved by making the Redeemer the general manager of the entire round of creation. By this means every intelligence learned to love and honor the great Jehovah.

Second, this much-loved person must go through a horrendous crisis of infinite agony and suffering which is so intense that it arouses an outcry of compassion in every single intelligence who belongs to this round of creation.

Third, this much-loved person must then require repentance and a complete surrender to the requirements of the gospel so that Jesus will intercede and petition for the sake of his suffering that the convert can return to the Father and continue on the pathway of eternal progression.

Therefore, to summarize: With each round of creation there has be an infinite sacrifice that arouses such a flood of mercy in the consciousness of every intelligence that it consents to permit the Father to bring us back into his presence so as to continue our training and exaltation.

Now we come to the climax of our discussion.

Who Should Put the Savior Through the Atoning Sacrifice?

In order provide a redemptive sacrifice, someone must slay the Savior under excruciating circumstances. Who should do this? Should it be planned in advance, or just left to chance and circumstances? No doubt this ugly question was discussed at length between the Father and the Son in the preexistence. We are led to presume that a discussion similar to the following dialogue must have taken place because that is exactly the way it turned out:

The Father: My son, as you know, with each new round of creation we have to choose someone to make a redemptive sacrifice. I am grateful that you volunteered to provide the needed sacrifice for this present round of creation. Now, whom are you planning to be responsible for bringing to pass your redemptive sacrifice? In other words, who should slay you?

The Son: I would like to have my redemptive sacrifice brought about by some of those who loved me and who valiantly supported me during the War in Heaven. Since I will be coming into mortality through the loins of David, I believe I would like to have the Jews bring about my crucifixion.

The Father: But they would never crucify you if they knew who you were. In fact, as Paul will later say, "Had they known it, they would not have crucified the Lord of Glory" (1 Corinthians 2:8).

The Son: Then I must arrange it so they will not realize who I am until after the crucifixion is over.

The Father: How will you bring that about?

The Son: Here is my plan. I will have the Jewish prophets reveal that the Messiah will be a Jew and that the Jews will think he is an impostor and slay him. Of course, their leaders will say that they would never kill their Messiah. No doubt they will denounce the prophecy as a myth and consider it an insult to the Jewish people. They will not only forbid anyone to preach this doctrine but pronounce a death penalty on anyone who dares to preach it. I am sure they will also remove from the scriptures the writings of any prophet who has taught that the Messiah will be killed by his own people. As a result of this, they will have no way of knowing who I am when I come among them as the Redeemer. They will only know about my Second Coming when I will come in power as the great King Messiah. As a result, when I come to the earth the first time, they will expect me to come in power and set up a worldwide Jewish kingdom. When this fails to materialize, they will think I am an impostor and allow me to be killed.

The Father: Then what will happen to those who consented to your death because they thought you were an impostor?

The Son: Since they merely assented to my death, thinking I was an impostor, they will not be guilty of murder. Therefore, they can be forgiven because of my atoning sacrifice which they themselves will have helped me bring about. After my resurrection I will explain to them that this was arranged in heaven before the world began. I will tell them that I wanted to have the Jews, my own people, assist in bringing about my sacrifice. Once it is explained to them how they innocently helped me through my redemptive ordeal, they can repent of their sins, including assenting to my death. I can then invite them to be baptized for the remission of their sins and welcome them into my kingdom.

The Father: But what about any of those who do not accept your invitation to enter your kingdom or still believe they assented to the crucifixion of an impostor?

The Son: They will be like anyone else who knowingly sins against the truth and rejects the message of the gospel. They will have to suffer the consequences.

The Father: I approve of the plan. It is identical with the one we have used in other rounds of creation throughout eternity.

Putting the Plan Into Operation

After the tribe of Judah came into existence around 1800 B.C., the prophets of Israel taught the people the fullness of the gospel and explained to them that there would be a Messiah who would serve as a mediator to secure the forgiveness of their sins.

This seemed to be understood and fully accepted, but around a thousand years later, when several prophets taught how the Jews would help Jesus through this ordeal they were stoned to death for preaching it.

This is what happened to the Prophet Zenos and Zenoch (Helaman 8:19) and in 600 B.C. when the prophet Lehi described his vision of the Savior being crucified at the instigation of the Jews in the meridian of time, he had to flee for his life. (1 Nephi 2:1-2)

Jesus Begins His Earthly Ministry

It is rather amazing but Jesus appeared in the Holy Land right about the time the Jews were expecting their King Messiah to arrive. This exciting anticipation was based on an erroneous interpretation of a prophecy in the second chapter of Daniel.

It will be recalled that around 625 B.C., King Nebuchadnezzar of Babylon had a terrible dream but could not afterwards remember it. The king threatened to execute all of his wise men if they did not tell him what the dream had been and what it meant. Daniel saved the lives of himself and three companions, as well as all of the king's wise men, by receiving a revelation from the Lord which told him what the king had dreamed and also what it meant.

The king had seen a huge, grotesque image in his dream. The image represented the future kingdoms that would rule the world. The head was of gold, which turned out to be Babylon itself. The chest and arms were of silver which turned out to be Persia that would conquer Babylon. The belly and thighs were of brass which turned out to be Greece that would conquer Persia. Then the hips and legs which were made of iron turned out to be the Romans who conquered Greece and later divided into the two legs of the eastern and western Roman Empires. The feet of the image were made of iron and miry clay which turned out to be the many European gentile nations which developed in more recent times after the Roman Empire collapsed.

Daniel then told Nebuchadnezzar that "in the days of these kings [those of iron and miry clay] shall the God of heaven set up a kingdom, which shall never be destroyed: and the kingdom shall not be left to other people, but it shall break in pieces and consume all these kingdoms and it shall stand forever." (Daniel 2:44)

Daniel had said that the final scenes of this vision would take place "in the latter days," (Daniel 2:28) but the Jews in the days of Jesus thought that since the cruel iron kingdom of Rome had already become established, the stone of God's kingdom should be coming forth shortly under the great Messiah. They felt it would not only destroy all of the existing worldly kingdoms, but last forever.

The Jewish rabbis were not willing to wait until the latter days but wanted to interpret the second chapter of Daniel as being fulfilled in their day. The supreme key to their distorted interpretation was the overthrow of the Romans. They therefore taught that no matter how many miracles Jesus might perform, if he did not overthrow the Romans, he was not the Messiah. So the people were waiting for Jesus to set up his kingdom and overthrow the Romans.

And we learn to our amazement that his apostles were expecting the same thing.

Why the Apostles Were Misled

We now know that it served the purposes of both the Father and the Son to have the apostles look upon Jesus as the King-Messiah.

It was by providential design, that all of the Jews – including the apostles – were allowed to think that Jesus had appeared on earth to fulfill the glorious prophecies of Daniel concerning the coming of the King-Messiah. After all, hadn't Jesus said: "I appoint unto you a kingdom. . .that ye may eat and drink at my table in my kingdom, and sit on thrones judging the twelve tribes of Israel." (Luke 22:29-30) And the mother of James and John was so completely certain Jesus was about to set up his kingdom that she requested the Savior to give her sons preferred treatment after he took over as the King-Messiah of the world. (Matthew 20:21-22)

The New Testament makes it clear that Jesus was successful in delivering his message without revealing the fact that he had come as the Redeemer rather than the King-Messiah. This was true even though Jesus spoke of his crucifixion and resurrection several times. Nevertheless, the Spirit hid it from the apostles and also those who considered themselves the Savior's disciples. Luke says, "And they understood none of these things, and THIS SAY-ING WAS HID FROM THEM." (Luke 18:34) We also have the statement of Mark who said: "They understood not that saying [about his death and resurrection] and were afraid to ask him." (Mark 9:32)

The assignment of the Holy Spirit was to erase from the minds of the apostles and the disciples of Jesus any reference to his death and resurrection. Speaking of Peter and John, the scripture says: "They knew not the scripture, that he would rise from the dead." (John 20:9) It was only after Jesus was glorified that the Spirit restored to their minds everything he had said concerning his crucifixion and resurrection during his ministry. (John 14:26)

The Savior's Heavy Burden

We do not know exactly when Jesus first learned during his earth life that he was to provide the Father's redemptive sacrifice.

We know that by the age of twelve Jesus knew that his real father was Elohim and that he should "be about his Father's business." (Luke 2:42-49) However, it is unlikely the Father would burden his son with a knowledge of the terrible ordeal that lay ahead of him until he had actually begun his mission in 30 A.D.

We speculate that a logical time for ministering angels to share the message of the redemptive sacrifice might have been right after his baptism. It will be recalled that immediately after his baptism he was quickened and led into the wilderness. There he received spiritual ministrations during forty days and forty nights. This would seem to have been the sacred interlude when ministering angels could have prepared Jesus for what lay ahead. It was a holy season of spiritual reinforcement when he survived six weeks without bread. (Luke 4:2)

Why Didn't the Jews Recognize Jesus?

Jesus performed his first spectacular miracle at the wedding feast in Cana and then prepared to go to Jerusalem when he would turn thirty years of age and be eligible, according to Jewish tradition, to launch his ministry.

Right from the beginning the ministry of Jesus was spectacular. He performed miracles by the hundreds. He healed the sick, raised the dead, walked on water, calmed turbulent seas, and fed hundreds of people with fish already cooked and bread already baked.

In fact, right from the beginning great throngs of Jews really did think Jesus was the Messiah, but the KING-Messiah. Their belief that he was the King-Messiah persisted right up to the last week of his life. But then their expectations collapsed.

By the end of the week he had not only failed to overthrow the Romans but the Romans had crucified him. Furthermore, Jesus suffered death when the students of the prophecy of Daniel had declared he would live forever.

Jesus Falters at the Last Supper

As Jesus drew near to the time of his betrayal he seemed engulfed by a dark and ominous shadow and could not avoid contemplating the horrible agony of the task that lay immediately before him. Finally he couldn't help telling his apostles that he was about to leave them.

Peter immediately wanted to know where he would be going. The chief apostle assured the Savior that no matter where he was going, Peter wanted to accompany him and protect him from the enemies that seemed to be increasing by the hour.

Jesus cut him short and said:

*"Wilt thou lay down thy life for my sake? Verily,
verily, I say unto thee, The cock shall not crow, till
thou hast denied me thrice."* (John 13:38)

This abrupt prediction could have been deeply offensive to
Peter and quite out of character for their loving Master. However,
Jesus knew that within a few hours Peter as well as all the other
disciples would have lost their testimonies and become totally
confused concerning his divinity.

In connection with his great High Priest prayer recorded by
John, Jesus said:

*"Father, the hour is come. . . And now, O Father,
glorify thou me with thine own self with the glory
which I had with thee before the world was."*

(John 17:1, 5)

Then he asked his apostles to accompany him to his favorite
place of prayer on Mount Gethsemane. By the time they reached
Gethsemane the apostles became alarmed with the drastic change
in the Savior's demeanor. It seemed as though a morbid depression
had settled on his spirit. He had always been so steadfast, so coura-
geous, and so full of self confidence. They had seen him defy
storms, walk on the sea, raise the dead, and cast out devils. They
had always been so proud of their King-Messiah. But now he had
changed and the disciples were shocked as his spirits crumbled
and he began acting like an ordinary frightened human being.
They heard him say:

*"My soul is exceeding sorrowful, even unto
death."* (Matthew 26:38)

All of this was so completely out of character for Jesus that the
inspired version says:

*"The disciples began to be sore amazed, and to be very
heavy and to complain in their hearts, WONDERING
IF THIS BE THE MESSIAH."* (JST Mark 14:36)

Their testimonies were crumbling.

The Savior Faces His Supreme Crisis

He left eight of the apostles at the garden gate to guard it while he prayed. Then he took Peter, James and John further up the Mount of Olives. There the apostles sat down and almost immediately went to sleep. But Jesus went off by himself and fell full length upon the ground. According to Mark 14:36 he cried out:

"Abba Father, ALL THINGS ARE POSSIBLE UNTO THEE. Take away this cup from me, nevertheless, not what I will but what thou wilt."

In other words, thou art God. You are all-powerful. Please work this out some other way. Don't make me go through with it.

At this moment the Father was suffering a pang of the deepest anguish. He knew the overwhelming torment through which Jesus was passing, but he also knew that unless he fulfilled his mission this whole round of creation would disintegrate and return to outer darkness. Of course, the Father knew the end from the beginning and realized that Jesus would persevere. But this knowledge did not diminish the penetrating anguish which he knew his Son was having to endure. He therefore sent an angel to comfort the Savior. (Luke 22:23) We don't know who he was but I would not be surprised if it turns out to be Adam or Michael.

We also don't know what he said, but we can well imagine that it might have gone something like this. "Jesus, you don't have to do this. You still have your free agency. But if you do not fulfill your calling, you ought to know what the consequence will be." He then may have described for Jesus the crash of this whole round of creation.

The Book of Mormon specifically describes what would have happened to the human family if there had been no Atonement (Mosiah 16:4-5) and we feel this merely represents what would happen to this entire round of creation. Concerning mankind, every one of us would suffer the same fate as Lucifer and his dark angels. We would have been disembodied and left without any tabernacle, either spiritual or physical. Then we would have been cast "back" into outer darkness as stripped, naked intelligences. (D&C 88:32;73)

And Brigham Young describes what would have happened to Jesus himself. He says:

> *"Jesus was foreordained before the foundations of the world were built, and his mission was appointed him in eternity to be the Savior of the world, yet when he came in the flesh he was left free to choose or refuse to obey the Father.*
>
> *"Had he refused to obey his Father he would have become a son of perdition."* (*Journal of Discourses*, vol. 10 p. 324)

This would mean that eventually Jesus would have followed the disembodied Lucifer and the rest of us into outer darkness.

But, praise be to God, Jesus chose the thorny pathway of terrifying torture for which he was born. He said to the Father: "Thy will be done." Even as he said it, a flood of total anguish flooded over him. As a result, he sweat great drops of blood. After the passion of it all had subsided, he awakened his apostles and went down toward the gate where Judas was already coming with the soldiers from the temple.

Events Leading Up to the
Apostles Losing Their Testimonies

Peter knew that Jesus did not have to be taken captive by the soldiers. All he had to do was disappear as he had done during crises on a number of occasions in the past. But he didn't disappear and when Peter saw that they were about to take him prisoner he drew out his sword and struck at Malchus, a relative of the high priest. The blade slid off the side of his head and sliced off the ear of Malchus. Jesus instantly healed it and told Peter to put up his sword. It all happened so quickly, Malchus probably never realized that a miracle had been performed. As the guards led Jesus away the apostles fled in all directions lest they be arrested as well.

Later, Peter and John went to the courtyard of the Sanhedrin where it was obvious the highest religious court in Israel was legally ensnaring Jesus so the Romans would crucify him.

Obviously Jesus was not going to overthrow the Romans. This would be the end of the hopes of the Jews. When a woman asked Peter if he were a disciple of Jesus, he denied it. Another woman asked him if he were a disciple of Jesus and he denied it. Finally, he was challenged by Malchus whose ear had been miraculously healed and this time Peter cursed and swore. He said he didn't know that man. Peter's world was crumbling to pieces. He had lost his testimony and it says he went out into the night and wept. (Matthew 26:73-75)

In no way would Peter have guessed the thrill that would animate his soul when he was suddenly visited by the resurrected Christ three days after his crucifixion. And fifty days later, at the celebration of the Feast of the Pentecost he would explain the Atonement of Christ to a large crowd of Jews and three thousand of them would apply for baptism. A short time later, he would give the same talk at the Temple and five thousand would apply for baptism. What a glorious message he had for all who would listen!

Jesus Saves Our Universe With His Life

Now we are confronted with one final challenge. How did the crucifixion of Jesus redeem mankind and save this whole round of creation?

There is only one place in the scripture where you can get the whole story. It is in Alma chapter 34 where Amulek the missionary companion of Alma explained it to the Zoramites. He begins with the surprising declaration that the suffering of Jesus was not to pay for our sins because one person cannot pay for the sins of another, but what Jesus did was to arouse the mercy and compassion in all the hosts of intelligences in our part of the universe so they would grant the Savior anything he asked for in righteousness. As Amulek points out, this means the Atonement was not based on justice – so much suffering for so much sin – but on the creation of a vast reservoir of mercy and compassion that would gain for us not only the forgiveness of sins but all of the gifts of eternal life and the upward ascent in our eternal progression.

There were two aspects of Christ's Atonement that only he could have fulfilled. First of all, the atoning sacrifice had to be

glorious planet Kolob. As the resurrected Jesus embraced the glorious resurrected Elohim, no doubt Jesus whispered into his father's ear: "I did it. I did it. I did it."

What a glorious achievement. The plan Jesus had proposed was a total victory for both the Father and the Son. Now you know why the Atonement was so essential to the Father as well as to us.

And may I close with my most solemn and sacred testimony that he did it. He did it.

In the name of Jesus Christ, Amen.

A basic illustration of SPACE and OUTER DARKNESS

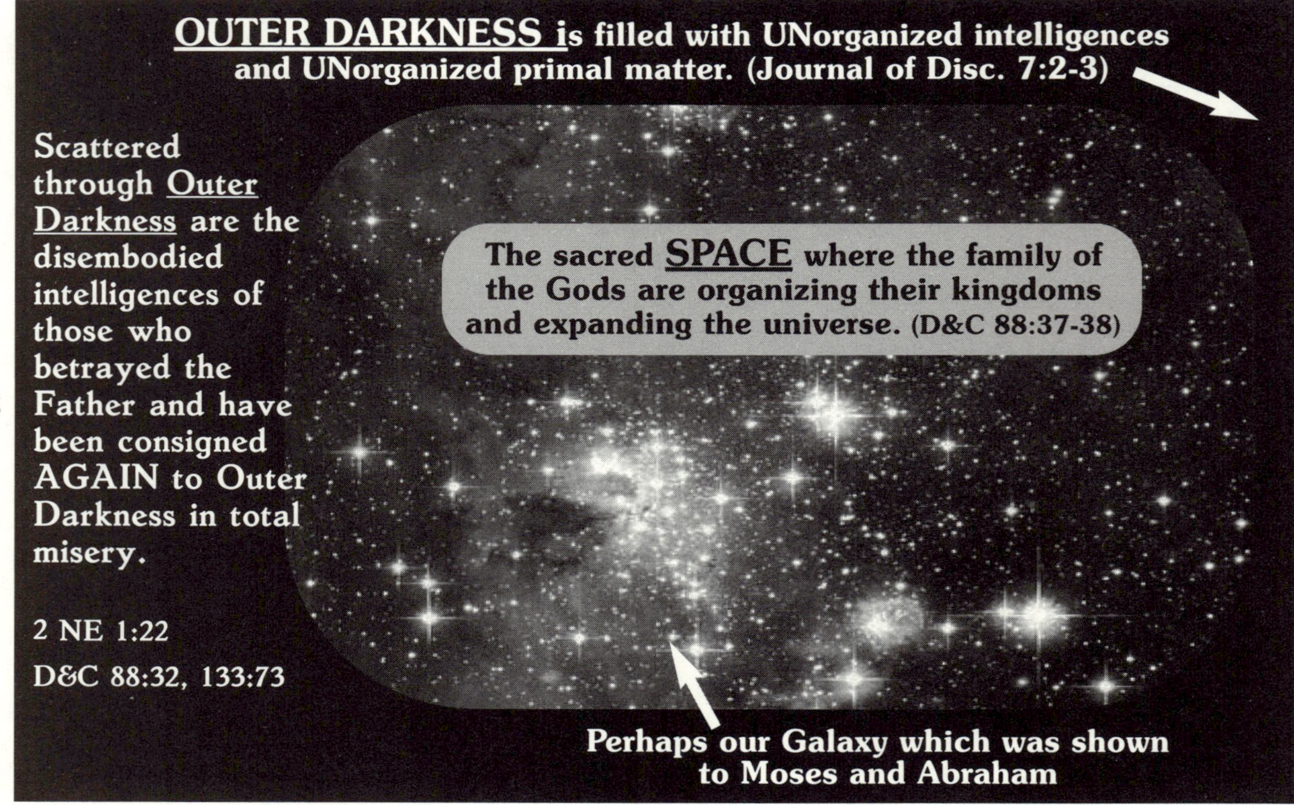

A Personal Search for
The Meaning of the Atonement

By W. Cleon Skousen

Transcribed and edited by Harold Skousen, © 2005 Ensign Publishing Co.

This transcript is from a talk given by W. Cleon Skousen in December of 1980 at an LDS Missionary Zone Conference in Dallas, Texas. Over 200 missionaries were in attendance. Some minor editing has been applied to make the presentation more readable.

My fellow missionaries,

I count this a great honor to have the privilege of spending a few minutes with you this beautiful day in Texas.

I think that one of the greatest blessings that come to a person in this life is the calling of a missionary.

Now, I can't help but think, and I won't tell you how long ago, what a challenging thing it was to come into the mission field. I'm sure it was an equally traumatic experience for you. You have loved ones at home that are praying for you and thinking about you and hoping that out there are some special people that our Heavenly Father has set up just waiting to hear your testimony and your knock at their door so that you will have the great thrill of sharing the treasure of the gospel with them.

I received my calling at the age of 17, along with one other 17 year-old missionary that I later became acquainted with from Arizona. We were two 17 year-olds that were allowed to go into the mission field that particular year.

In order to go on a mission I had worked here in Texas, part of the time, at a dollar a day and my board driving four mules on a Fresno in order to save up the necessary funds in order to go.

Because I was sent to England and my father had to pay the way, he had to sell his favorite team of horses so that I could go.

Everything was just great! It was so exciting—I got a new suit (but just one!) a new pair of shoes and a new outfit. That was precious money that I spent for it.

It was so exciting going over on the boat with the former Prime Minister from Canada on a boat called the Empress of Australia. We sailed out of Quebec, Canada, and then hit the storms in the North Atlantic Sea. We were all ill for about four days.

Finally we landed in Plymouth, England, and taken to downtown London where the Mission Headquarters was located. By the time I got to London, I was a very home-sick 17 year-old boy. I was a "man" when I left home, but when I hit London I was a "boy." I didn't see anything that looked familiar to me at all, except a Kellogg's Cornflakes sign!

When I got on the train and they asked me for my fare. I said to the conductor, "How much is it?" and he answered, "A couple a' bob n' tuppance a'pney." I had just changed a five dollar bill into British currency, so I reached in my pocket, held out the money and hoped he was honest. I had no idea what he was talking about.

So I traveled up to the London Mission Headquarters. Most of the Elders that came over with me had been to college somewhat and they knew all the other fellows. I was a missionary from California, and in those days there weren't very many missionaries going on missions. I didn't know anybody. So they were all fraternizing and "how-to-doing." I kind of enjoyed it the first 15 or 20 minutes. But after a while I got a little lonesome.

I was sitting over on a couch all by myself, when a great big Elder came over to me and said, "Elder Skousen?"

I said "Yes!"

He said, "I'm Elder Doan from Arizona."

I replied, "Hi."

He said, "I know a lot of Skousen's in Arizona." I told him Arizona is family headquarters, but I was from California.

He said, "How would you like to be my companion tonight and go out on a street meeting at Hyde Park? My companion is ill and I thought maybe you'd like to go."

I said, "Well, do I have to speak?"

He said, "No, you wouldn't have to speak. I just need to have somebody with me." I replied that I would like to go.

Elder Doan then went over into a closet, reached down and picked up what looked like a bag of sticks—long round sticks wrapped in a canvas. He took his briefcase and said, "Follow me."

We walked over and got onto the "Underground Railroad" as they called it. Pretty soon we got off the train and came up. He said, "This is Hyde Park."

Amazing! Thousands of people all milling around—over here was a communist talking against the government; here was the Salvation Army band playing so loud you couldn't hear yourself think; over there was someone else talking about their religion, etc. Thousands of people were all milling around listening to speakers. Some even selling quack medicine. Everything was going on there.

And here is Elder Doan—he just went right into the middle of that crowd and he would say, "Pardon me please. Pardon me, pardon me." He was looking at the sidewalk for something. I didn't know what he had lost, but he was looking for something.

"Pardon me, pardon me." He was looking for a little brass number which had been assigned to him for two hours.

Finally he located it and said, "Would you excuse me please. Excuse me. Would you move back please just a little." He then got down, unwrapped his canvas sack, and got out his sticks. I didn't know if he was going to build a fire or what. But he started putting them together like tinker toys. The next thing I knew he had a little platform. It had four legs on it with a little stand up in front. He then flipped over a piece of canvas on top and it said, "Mormons: The Church of Jesus Christ of Latter-day Saints."

He reached into his briefcase, pulled out a steal plate and put that across the four legs. Elder Doan was about 200 pounds and 6 foot something. And he got up on that platform! I held my breath—it seemed to hold.

By this time I looked out at the crowd. A lot of people, just as though they had expected him, were all turning toward him. Elder Doan stood up there and towered over the audience. I thought, "This is really exciting."

He then turned to me, took off his hat, handed it to me, and there all by himself he stood there and began singing, "How Firm a Foundation." Now that was rather interesting!

Then he began his talk, which lasted 40 minutes. I was so proud of him—everybody was listening intently. When he finished he asked the crowd if there were any questions. There was a little fellow standing right in front of him dressed in a cut-away coat and striped trousers. He had been so nervous during the talk. He could just hardly wait for questions. He looked like he was somebody—he had a top-hat and everything. So right away he said, "Elder, Elder." Those are the kind you have to always take care of first.

So Elder Doan said, "Yes, my good man."

This fellow said, "I've been listening to the Mormon Elders for nigh onto twenty years, and I have never heard from a Mormon Elder who didn't come from the 'great walled City of Salt Lake.' What I would like to hear, is an Elder who doesn't come from the 'great walled City of Salt Lake.'"

I thought to myself, "Elder Doan comes from Arizona. He'll take care of this real well."

So Elder Doan turned to the crowd and said, "How many of you would like to hear from a Mormon Elder who does not come from the 'great walled City of Salt Lake?'" The whole crowd cheered, "Here-here! Here-here!"

He said, "I have with me tonight [a little pause] a young man who has only been on British soil upwards of five hours or so. He is from America and he comes from near Hollywood." (I actually live in San Bernardino—60 miles away from Hollywood—but they wouldn't know about San Bernardino.)

Elder Doan continued, "I promised him because he is just new that I wouldn't call upon him to speak. But since YOU have asked him to speak, I will introduce to you Elder Skousen."

There have only been a few times in my life when I have been so frightened that I've been paralyzed—and this was one of them! It put a shock through me I will never forget. I was almost in a stupor as he pushed me forward onto that little stand. That was the shakiest stand you ever saw! There was nothing firm about its foundation when I got on it!

What was worse, I didn't know what to say. So I just stood there looking at the crowd. I thought of Primary, Sunday School. There must have been something somewhere I've learned. I thought of the Mission Home in Salt Lake—what do I say, what should I say! The Spirit then finally came to my rescue and said, "Tell them why you are here." I thought to myself, "That's a good question!"

Anyway, I finally got my wits enough so that I could talk. I began telling them that something wonderful had happened. It could have happened in England or in Denmark from which my people came. But it didn't. It happened in America—and if it had happened in England we would have expected you to come over to America and tell us about it. Since this great thing happened in America, we have come clear over here to tell you. The more I thought about it the more exciting it got. I lasted ten minutes, bore my testimony and started to step down.

But there was that little fellow in the cut-way coat: "Elder! Elder!"

I replied, "Yes, sir."

He said, "Would you give me the Mormon interpretation of II Kings 11 and 12 compared to Acts 9 and 3?"

Hmmm, 2nd Kings. I thought hard. Hmmm, there were kings in the Book of Mormon. I didn't even know for sure which standard works the book of Kings was in! I really didn't. So I finally gave him the answer they told us to use in the Mission Home.

I said, "Now, if I am here a week from tonight, when this meeting is held again, I will carefully study those passages so that I can correctly present the Church's position on them. So if I am here, I promise I will do that next time and thank you very much." I got down off that stand so fast! Elder Doan got back up—and I thought he would answer that question—but no sir, that's my question! He's not going to answer my question. He just went on to something else.

Well, that's how that evening ended.

However, a week later I was not in London. I had been assigned to Sheffield, in the middle of Yorkshire. I thought I had come to an English speaking country but this area was totally hostile to me. It was a smoky city where they made steel and I just could not understand the people. You might think Texans are hard to understand sometimes—you ought to be in Yorkshire. They have a little saying that goes something like this:

"An' if tha does owt for nowt, do it for thysen tha noth." That's old English—very old English.

It means, "If you do anything for nothing, do it for yourself, ladi."

"An' if tha does owt for nowt, do it for thysen tha noth." You try and teach the Gospel and have that dialogue with Mr. Brown on that basis—what a challenge.

So that is how my mission began. It was a marvelous experience. I was frightened from the moment I arrived in the mission field until I came home. It was just one big challenge after another.

The biggest challenge of all came when I was asked to preside over Ireland—beautiful Ireland. I didn't even expect to become a senior companion being so young. But the mission president said, "We are going to send you up to Ireland. We just had five of our missionaries mobbed and thrown into the bay. Even Elder Doan was badly hurt. So we are going to send you up there. You go in to see the Chief of Police and tell him we're back!"

At any rate, we had six marvelous months in Belfast, Ireland. We did everything they told us to do, and we didn't get mobbed. As a matter of fact, we were very careful about how we presented it: First at the Custom House steps. As our crowds got much bigger, we had to meet at the place in Belfast where the five streets come together. The police provided us with a piano box on which we could stand so we would be high enough to talk to the people. Eventually we were able to use the largest hall in Belfast for our big Conference in the fall.

When I was later ready to leave on a boat for home, the saints came down to the dock to tell me goodbye. The captain came over to me asked me to come up higher so the other people could see me. I said, "What other people?" He said, "Those other people down on the peer. They want you to come up on higher deck to see you." I was confused but followed him anyway. When I got up to the higher deck, the whole peer was full of people and they began to sing, "God Be With You Till We Meet Again." I just stood there and cried like a baby.

I thank my Heavenly Father that I had that marvelous blessing of coming on a mission, and having all those scary experiences. You just never know what is going to happen to you. If you just keep working vigorously and pushing forward, the Lord will bless you.

Now, that earlier question: "Why are you here?" Tell them why you came on a mission. "What are you doing out here in the mission field—what are you doing trembling on this little stand? Tell them what you came for."

It took me a long time, really, to find out why I was there. I could testify of the Restoration—but that you see isn't our main message. The restoration is only incidental. We have a bigger testimony than that, and there isn't any better time than Christmas time to remind ourselves what our message really is.

I finally became resolved on my mission and got to studying the scriptures. I was so scared after that experience in Hyde Park. I read from Genesis to Revelations like I was going to be asked about every passage at every street meeting from then on. I read it frantically. I gulped it. I underlined it, marked it, re-read it. It was a desperation reading. I then did the same thing to the Book of Mormon, the Doctrine and Covenants, and Pearl of Great Price. I began to get the thrill of it all and resolved I would not stop studying when I got home. Resolve to stay with your studies after you get off your mission. Finish your college, get into family life, get into your professional life and keep close to the Lord and the scriptures.

As I used to say to my BYU students when we were studying the Book of Mormon together, "Always say your prayers before you start studying." We had a study course that required you to fill in blanks. First you read a chapter, and then fill in the blanks. Often you would have to read the chapter again because you can't remember the key blank answer. The study course included a blank for every verse—a key word in each verse. I taught them to carefully and methodically study these treasures from the Book of Mormon, and every once in a while you will find yourself crying. When that happens to you, you must realize that is the Lord talking to you and saying, "This is true, this is all true."

You might wonder why you are crying—you feel so good, what are you crying for? When that happens, get on your knees immediately. Just kneel there and say, "Thank you, Heavenly Father, for talking to me." That's what made you cry. When the Spirit of the Lord talks to you, it will often make you cry. You need to recognize that.

It used to thrill me when sometimes a big football player or someone would stay until all the class was gone. A bit embarrassed about it, but they would say, "Brother Skousen, it happened to me. Just this week while I was studying it happened. My, it was great— just great." I would say, "Thank you for sharing that with me." He would reply, "I thought it would never happen to me. But it really did." Now that's the Spirit talking to you. Once that conversion has started working in your heart, then marvelous things start happening to you. Your mind begins to open up and you begin getting answers to questions.

That brings me to the next thing I want to talk about.

I have always been puzzled, as a boy, by the Easter story. I used to sit there in Sunday School in Raymond, Alberta, Canada, and they told me how Jesus suffered on the cross. That just left a lot of questions in my mind.

Here is a beautiful, beautiful person—the son of our Heavenly Father—he's up on that cross. He has a crown made of thorns on his; dried blood down his face. He's been all lacerated by a cat-of-nine-tails. He's got spikes in his hands and in his wrists and in his feet. He is all sweaty and bloody and he hanging there on the cross.

I wanted to know what that's for. I wanted to know what that does. What does that help do? And who wanted that anyway? Everybody says its necessary, I want to know why and what it accomplishes and what he's doing up there. The Romans crucified a lot of people, but why the son of God? What was this for? Why was this prophesied—did Enoch say he would die on a cross? I used to say that every Easter.

So when I got on my mission, age 17, I'm riding on a train in England with an apostle of the Lord, John A. Widstoe. He was sitting there like all mission presidents do, worrying about the conference with the missionaries and so on. He was very quiet and meditative when I leaned over and said, "Brother Widtsoe, can I ask you a question?" He seemed a bit startled and looked up at me and said, "Yes?" I knew I had suddenly awakened him from a revere of meditation on something. Elder Widtsoe was also a very famous scientist.

I said to him, "I just wanted to ask you about why the Atonement was necessary. I accept the fact this it is, but I just wondered why. I wondered what caused it to have the Father require the Son to go through this."

Brother Widtsoe thought a moment and then replied, "Elder Skousen, who asked you to ask me this question?"

I answered, "Well, nobody. It's my question. Nobody asked me to ask it."

He said, "I'm not asked that question very often. Do you really want to know why the Atonement was necessary?"

I replied, "Well, if it's alright."

"Yes," he said. "It's alright. How badly do you want to know the answer?"

I said, "Well, I've wanted to know it ever since I was a little boy."

Brother Widtsoe said, "Alright. You know, if people don't ask questions, they can't hear the answer." He continued, "So I will share the answer with you over a period of time."

I told him I really appreciated that, and got out my pencil told him that if he would give me the verses I would right them down.

He said, "Well, I will tell you what to look for and I'll tell you which standard work its in." I asked, "aren't' you going to give me the chapter and verse?"

He answered, "I wouldn't deprive you of the thrill of finding it."

So he told me what to look for, and what the source of God's power was—and this is where you'll find it in the early part of the Doctrine and Covenants. And here is where Jesus asked if he couldn't get out of it, and this is in several passages in the New Testament. It will say these things and you look for that. Then you will find some very basic scientific truths located in Second

Nephi and here is what it will tell you.

Did you know it took me seven years before I had located all those passages! Each time I would thereafter see Elder Widtsoe both on and off my mission I would report in.

He would say, "Well, you are doing pretty good. I'll give you the section of D&C. Try 88 or 29 or whatever it was. So I would look, and there it was-there it was! I had read right past it several times and missed it.

Finally I had it all written up, put it together and sent him a copy. He said, "Alright now, we need to get some of these things back into the main stream of thought because the Latter-day Saints aren't doing what the prophet Jacob said to do." He said we ought to talk more about the Atonement and why it is necessary. He asked me to put this in my next book, which I did in the "First 2000 Years" in the appendix: "Why Is the Atonement Necessary?"

The story begins with the shepherds watching their flocks on that April evening, 2000 years ago. Listen to the angels when they appeared to the shepherds.

The fact that Jesus was about to be born wasn't the important thing. Just being born wasn't important. It was early in the spring, in April. It wasn't December 25th, that's when the Romans were celebrating the birth date of Sol, their sun god. The Christians didn't have a birth date for Jesus, so they used the convenience of the Roman holiday for Sol. That's how it came to be the 25th of December. There aren't any sheep out in December—they are out in the spring when the grass is starting. That starts in the second week of March, so that's why the shepherds were out there.

So they are watching their sheep—lots of wolves out there in those days, that's why their watching them. Then all of the sudden it happened. Here's this burst of light and a personage appears. He realized he had scared them. Joseph Smith said when I prayed and Moroni came, I was expecting something to happen. But even so, when he came he had to comfort him. The first thing Moroni said to him was not to be afraid.

So this is what the angles said to the shepherds, "Fear not.

For behold, I bring you good tidings of great joy; which will be to all people. For unto you is born this day in the city of David, a Savior which is Christ the Lord. And this shall be a sign unto you; ye shall find him wrapped in swaddling clothes, lying in a manger."

Then the heavenly choirs couldn't be held back. They split back the veil and sang until music just filled the skies. They repeated one sentence over and over--enough for the shepherds to remember: "Glory to God in the highest. And on earth peace, good will toward men."

Now, I think maybe we were there. I'm sure the saints from Adam on down were there—maybe those of us who hadn't been on the earth yet weren't allowed to be there. But a lot of people were there and they sang!

Just prior to this event, it was exciting to be in that great Heavenly conference. This was just before Jehovah had appeared to Nephi II the day before and said he was going to come in the flesh tomorrow and tonight would be the sign.

So there he is, telling us all good bye as he is about to go down to the amnesia of the second estate. He won't even know who he is. You don't even know who you are. I don't even know who I am—isn't that exciting?

Now Jesus is brought into this world and is carefully raised by Joseph and Mary. By time he was twelve he had been ministered to by angels and they had told him who he really was.

He had seen enough visions and revelations so that he could pick up Isaiah, he could explain Jeremiah, and Ezekiel, and converse with the most learned scribes there in Solomon's porches on the Temple square. And he would say what Isaiah really saw.

The priests were fascinated. A twelve year-old boy who hadn't even been to the school of Gamael, yet he knew all the answers to all these mystical scriptures they had studied so hard to try and understand.

By the time Jesus was thirty, he was ready for the ministry. Having had some marvelous experiences, he is still learning about himself. In fact, when he would get wonderful things like Lazarus rising from the dead, he would say, "thank you Father, thank you." Then he would cry. "You did it for me, thank you father," and he'd cry. He was just kind of learning what it was like to be the son of God and have these wonderful powers.

But as the Savior approached the day of that great final Gethsemane, it shook him. He thought he was equal to it. He was doing pretty good, right up to the time of the last supper, when Judas would leave him.

Jesus was pretty sad, and was looking around the table. He said to his disciples that one of them would betray him. In shock, Peter said to John, "Ask him which one!" So John the Beloved asked Jesus, "Which one?"

Jesus replied, "He to whom I give the sap." He then took some bread, dipped it into the gravy and handed it to Judas, saying, "Whatsoever thou do'ist do thou quickly." It was beginning to get to Jesus. He had already washed their feet and taught them the sacred ordinance of the sacrament

But as soon a Judas went out, Jesus stood up and gave that great High Priest prayer found in John 17, "And now Father, neither pray I for these alone but for them also which shall believe on them through their words that they all might be one as thou Father art in me and I in thee. That they also may one in us." What a great prayer.

Then he said to his disciples, "I must go pray, I must pray." So he and the 11 disciples went from the upper room and apparently across the Temple square and down through the golden gate, across brook Kidren where we have walked so many times—I visited it for the 30th time here in October. He went on up into the groves of the olive trees. Then something interesting happened.

Eight disciples he had waiting sort of at the gateway—and they immediately fell asleep. He went further up the hill and had the three remaining apostles wait there. Apparently John was the only one who stayed awake, as far as we know. At least he is the only one that recorded the details of what we know about what happened. And it says that Jesus went and threw himself full length—he didn't kneel at a rock or a tree. He just threw himself on the ground.

Now, Brothers and Sisters, I would like you to take out a piece of paper so that you won't have to search for seven years for some of these choice, choice passages. I want you to write down first of all: Mark 14:36.

This is where Jesus says to his father, "Oh Father, all things are possible unto thee." In other words, "you are God the Father. You can do anything. You have it within your power." Then came the Saviors petition to his father, "Take this cup from me."

He is saying: "work it out some other way. Please do it without my having to go through with this." He was trembling. But the Father knew there wasn't any other way. All things are indeed possible unto God. However, he is a God of law. He is a God of cause and effect. He is a God of love and a God of justice. But what the Son had been called to do is the only way—there isn't any other way.

So the Father had to send an angel sown to Jesus. I wish we had that conversation in the scriptures. We can only guess what the angel might have said. But he did minister to Jesus, and he probably said to him:

"You don't have to do this. Everybody has their free agency. But the Father knew you would do it, and that's why you were ordained from the preexistence. The Father knew you would complete this brutal assignment. But you don't have to—it is your choice. But if you don't do it, everything in which your hand participated by way of creation will go back to outer chaos: the earth, the animals, the plants, the human beings and their bodies, all the other planets on which there are similar families that you helped to create. They all eventually go back to chaos. The only way they can be preserved and perpetuated and exalted, is to have you do this." The angel probably said something like that. At least he convinced the Savior that he must go forward if he wanted the Father's will to be done.

That is when the Savior said, "Thy will be done." And then, "He sweat great drops of blood."

Now let me give you the other passages that fill in these details:

Matthew 26:39. "Let this cup pass from me."

Luke 22:43. "The angel came and ministered to him."

Luke 22:44. As soon as he had said "They will be done," the

terror of the assignment came upon him with such an overwhelming impact, that the capillaries of his circulatory system couldn't even contain his blood. And it came through the sweat glands onto his skin as it were, great drops of blood.

That is the kind of suffering you and I couldn't even contemplate, let alone endure. But he did. And then he said in Matthew 26:42, "Thy will be done."

One of the things that you learn in studying the scriptures is to get all of the authorities who talk on the same incident. Take all of the details that each of them have, and then piece them together so that you've got the whole picture. And that's the one we have here.

Jesus describes his terror in Doctrine and Covenants 19:15-19. We'll read that in a moment.

In Acts 4:12, we are told that the Father himself could not have saved us. There is only one name given under Heaven whereby you can be saved and it is not Elohem. I don't know if this disturbs you or not. I thought God could do anything. Why couldn't he save us after we have fallen? Does that question bother you a little? That's the one I asked Brother Widtsoe. Doesn't God love us as much as the Son? After all, it is His plan to have us come down here.

Why is there only one name given under Heaven whereby we can be saved and it doesn't include the Father, only the Son. Is there an answer to that?

"Yes," Brother Widtsoe said. "There is an answer." (He didn't tell me it would take seven years for me to totally figure that out!)

Well, that raises all the questions. Now let's look for some answers.

Brother Widtsoe didn't give me these answers the way I have lined them up here. He gave me some of the big answers first. But I want to start with one of the fundamental answers, which is the bottom line of where it all happens.

Turn to 2 Nephi 2:14.

Father Lehi is on his death bed. He is trying to share with his sons the last element of Gospel testimony before he passes away. He is pleading with his sons to acknowledge and recognize the great truths of the Gospel.

He says we must realize that there is a God, and that he created everything either to act or be acted upon.

Now, there are two building blocks in the universe.

One building block consists of an active ingredient. It acts.

There is another thing that does not act, but it can be acted upon. You've read that passage in 2 Nephi. I had read it. I have gone through the Book of Mormon as a teacher over one hundred times--either teaching it or studying it, over one hundred times. It's like what President Matheny mentioned this morning, "People keep adding things to the Book of Mormon for me. I keep finding new things!" Well, this is one new thing that Brother Widtsoe pointed out to me.

He said it is there, just look for it in the early part of 2 Nephi—and there it was: "something to act and something to be acted upon."

Now turn to D&C 93:30.

That which "acts," the Lord says, is called "intelligence" or "light." So we ask, what then is "an intelligence?"

There is no description, except that it's like "light." And everything that exists, which is "truth," is filled with intelligence. Everything is filled with it.

Perhaps the best way for you to know about "intelligence" is to find out about it the way I found out about it. I said to Brother Widtsoe, "What is "an intelligence" like?"

He said to me, "Well, look in the mirror and tell him—you are an intelligence. "Oh that's right, that's good! Yes, I am an intelligence." I said.

Then he asked, "How big are you? Where are you?"

I said I'm right here. "No," he said, "you're not down there—did you notice? Isn't that down from where you are? Take a hold of your chin and shut your eyes. Is that below you or above you? Now take hold of your ears. Is that beside you? Where is your little 'I Am'?"

I replied, "Its way in there isn't it?"

He said, "I think so. It's a little tiny "I Am.' It is self knowing, self determining, anticipatory, and it can learn. It is a little intelligence."

Fascinating! And this little intelligence has always existed as an independent entity—a little "I Am."

Turn now to D&C 93:29-30.

This scripture tells us that "intelligence" is eternal and it is independent to act for itself. The Lord says this is the essence of reality that intelligence acts for itself.

Abraham 3:19-23. Here it talks about "spirits" and that some are more intelligent than others. Then it explains that spirits are organized intelligences. So actually we are talking about intelligences that are one above another. Intelligences are organized and graded.

What the Lord is saying here is that we start out with the little ones until we come up and here you are some of my most magnificent intelligences that I gave bodies in my image. You are marvelous and very special to Him.

In the Documentary History of the Church (DHC) volume 4, page 519, Joseph Smith described the graduated intelligences that are structured in nature. He mentions that he gave this sermon to the Apostles and their wives so they would know this wonderful, marvelous God science of graduated intelligence. Then he didn't say any more about it, so we have to read from the early Brethren who heard it, to get more details.

That which is "acted upon" is called "element" as found in D&C 93:33.

In the Journal of Discourses (JD) volume 7, page 2, Brigham Young says these little bits of element are "capacitated to receive intelligence."

Notice what happens. You get a little piece of element (and it must be extremely tiny), and you attach a little intelligence to it. Now you can talk to it. You can say, "Move that little fellow over here. Now you two combine together. Now bring in 3 more." Finally we have ourselves a little atom.

We get enough atoms together and we finally form a molecule. It is a universe of thousands or millions of tiny elements all spinning around in that little universe. We call it an atom—so tiny we can't see it! We put a lot of them together and we get a molecule. And these elements will do certain things.

The Lord says in D&C 88 that he gives these entities orders and then a pattern that they must follow. And they will always follow that pattern—unless you want them to do something different. So you get two little molecules that we call hydrogen, and another molecule that acts completely different, called oxygen, put them together and you've got water! Isn't that nice, you've got water.

But Jesus said, "Wine. You know what to do. A high grade of wine please." And it happens.

Now, all of the sudden the mystery has gone out of the miracles.

You and I achieve things by using force-against-force. That's the way you make a engine work—you explode something and those forces respond. But the Lord talks to things. That's a better way, wouldn't you agree?

God does not violate law. He sets things going. So you take Hydrogen plus Oxygen and you have created water. The Lord said "But I need wine." And the elements respond.

That's the universe in which we live. This is what we call "God Science."

Elder Widtsoe said, "Isn't that thrilling Elder Skousen?"

I replied "I never even thought of that being a possibility." He said that God has revealed so many marvelous things to us, if we will just study it out and put it all together.

Open up to Abraham 4:9, 10, 12 and 18.

Here we see intelligence responding to the commandments of the Gods during the creative process. Watch what it says:

"And the Gods command that the dry land to come up. And they watched until they were obeyed."

Now, dirt doesn't obey as dirt—unless it had intelligence in it, would it? If its just stuff, it has no capacity to obey.

This is one of the great revelations of God. These little intelligences are in everything. I can move a mountain, I just tell it to move. I can let my priesthood to tell it to move and if it's authorized, it will move.

Nephi II was told that the Lord declared before all his angels, that when you speak, Nephi, all things are to obey you as though God had spoken it. And I know that I can share this power with you because you will never use it until I tell you to. And he could say to the clouds, "Don't rain. Go away." Or you could say, "Clouds, come in. Let us have rain." That is the "power" of God.

Jesus would come and say to the little cells of the eyes, "You have not functioned properly since the birth of this man. In your places, please." And the man says, "I can see!"

"Crooked arm. Straighten!" And they are straightened.

"Feet. Walk!" And everything goes into its proper order and we call these "miracles." It is actually the science of God speaking to his creations saying "straighten up and fly right like you were supposed to!" That is what he is doing. This is the key to the miracles!

Helaman 12:3-18.

When God commands, they obey. Here it describes all the things that obey on Gods command. They obey just like they did during the creation process.

Jacob 4:6 and 1 Nephi 20:13

Jacob says we can have the water obey us; even trees obey us when we speak with the priesthood.

D&C 88:38-42. The Lord says "intelligence cleaveth unto intelligence" to do the things God has commanded it to do.

Now we come to a most interesting passage, hidden away, it took me a long time to discover it. I read over it at least ten or fifteen times. Brother Widtsoe said, "You're missing it in Section 29." He told me to read it again. I still couldn't find it and he said you need to "get the Spirit" when you read. Maybe you'll get it this time.

I finally got it! D&C 29:36.

Here God explains that his "honor" is his "power." Do you want to know where God got his power from? He said it is my "honor" that gives me my "power." My honor gives me power.

Brother Widtsoe said that this is a priesthood principle that often is not quite appreciated: "You are ordained from above; your power comes from that over which you have supervision."

What makes a great Bishop? His ordination? He is ordained from above, isn't he? But what makes him a great Bishop? It is Home Teachers home teaching; Sunday School teachers preparing their lessons; it is families holding Home Evenings, paying their tithes, and going to the Temple. And people say, "My, what a great Bishop!"

Why? Because he is being honored in his calling. That's what makes a great Bishop. He was ordained from above; he is supported from those below that he supervises. Do you follow that?

My honor is my power. "Water, change to wine"

When God appeared to Moses on Mount Sinai, Moses was 80 years old. Sinai means "the burning bush" and it was here that God appeared to him and said that he was now ready to rescue Israel out of Egypt.

Moses was so excited to hear this because he had his sister Miriam, his mother and even Aaron still being held captive in Egypt. Then the Lord said "I am going to have you, Moses, bring them out."

Moses replied, "No, no. I am a capital fugitive. They would kill me." The Lord said he would be with him, but Moses was still fearful.

So the Lord said, "What do you have there in your hand, Moses?" It was his shepherd staff. "Throw it on the ground, Moses." He threw it on the ground. It suddenly became a serpent; a metamorphosis had taken place. The Lord said, "Pick it up." So he did—by the tail of course. And it again became a staff.

Now watch what the Lord explained to Moses. "You see that hand? Do you want to see the miracle of God? That hand is made of dirt. Isn't that fantastic? That hand is made of dirt!"

The Lord said to Moses to put his hand in his bosom. So he did, and the Lord talked to that hand. He said: "Now my children don't go all the way back, let's go back to leprosy. Simulate leprosy. Moses, take your hand out."

As he did, it was now dripping with an incurable disease. "Moses, put your hand back in your bosom." The Lord said, "My children, as you were."

"Moses, take your hand back out." Pink, beautiful flesh!

Isn't that marvelous? And the Lord said to Moses if he wanted to take water and pour it out and have it be blood, I'll do that for you. "That they know that you come to them not by your own strength only, but by the very power of God."

Finally, Moses consented to go back into Egypt.

Once we begin to understand some of these principles, we begin to comprehend a little bit about the God we worship. That is really what the Lord is saying to us: "I want you to understand more about me. I want you to understand that I am not way off a mystical being. I am your loving Heavenly Father. I operate in an atmosphere of cause and effect. In the universe of laws, there is nothing magic about what I do. Everything I do is based on a science and I'm trying to teach it to you gradually."

We are told that God must maintain the confidences of these intelligences in order that they will sustain him and honor him.

No other Church on the earth has even dared to preach this doctrine (and no other scripture contains it, save the Book of Mormon), that it is possible for God to fall.

Now he isn't going to fall because he knows how to avoid it. He just wants us to know that he walks a razors edge of necessity of having his conduct as the great arbiter of Heaven, in whom they all love and respect—absolutely immaculate in dispensing justice and truth and his love among them.

Now that certainly is a great discipline, is it not?

In the passages Alma 42:13, 22, and 25, plus Mormon 9:19, we read,

". . .or he would cease to be God."

Who dares preach such a principle? God is under the necessity of maintaining certain conditions or he could cease to be God! He wouldn't have power any more.

How could be loose his power? By not being honored any more.

Now, we have the dilemma with the Atonement.

Our Father wanted us to come into a laboratory where good and evil existed side by side. Where you and I could learn for ourselves—not because Father said so—but we could learn for ourselves the difference between good and evil. And perhaps you noticed that a little evil seems to rub off onto us from time to time. In fact we have to repent and erase it continually. It keeps rubbing onto us! You think you've just about got the problem whipped, and the next thing you know you are doing it or tempted to do it again. That's life!

This is how we learn the difference between good and evil and the penalties thereof. We never went through this before. You learned how to be obedient in Heaven because our Heavenly Father told us what the results would be if we didn't obey. But we couldn't quite understand. He gave us the criteria but we couldn't know for ourselves, as the Book of Mormon explains. That is why we came into this life. We are really learning for ourselves.

Alma 34: 9 explains that the Father can not save us—the Atonement is indispensable. We have to have an Atonement.

But what would have happened if there had never been any Atonement?

Look in 2 Nephi 9:7-9.

We all would have become subject to Lucifer and suffer the same consequences (which the early Brethren made very clear) was total dissolution. This means they are stripped of their spirit body and they are stripped of all things that pertain to the organized kingdom of God. They are then cast back into outer darkness naked: A naked intelligence; unorganized.

The early Brethren in Joseph Smiths day thought maybe these unorganized intelligences might get another chance. They could possibly be scooped up again and come into another round of creation.

But then the Lord said in the Doctrine and Covenants, don't ever preach that they ever get a second chance. He has never authorized it to be taught that they get another chance. So we don't preach that.

So how does the Atonement work?

Alma 34:11. We have the problem, and now we have the basic ingredients for the solution. Here in Alma it explains that "one person can not pay for the sins of another." This was the prophet Amulec talking (not Alma). Amulec is a new convert to the Church and a missionary companion to Alma, as he is speaking to the Zoramites. Amulec explains that one person can not satisfy the demands of justice by paying for the sins of another.

You stop and think, and see if this is not true.

Let's say I have committed a heinous, capital offense. This good Elder sitting down here has offered to give his life on behalf of my offense, for which I should actually die. But he explains that Brother Skousen still has got a lot of teaching to do, so "I will go on the gallows for him, so he can live."

Does that satisfy any of you? Do you feel good about that? Are you satisfied? Do you feel justice has been done? Has it satisfied your sense of justice?

Amulec explains, "No, it will not."

Now this is a very important thing to understand about the Atonement. I keep hearing people preach, "Well, for this much sin there must be this much suffering, and that is what Jesus provided.

No, that is the law of "quid pro quo."

Amulec says the Atonement is based on a completely different principle.

It is not "quid pro quo." It isn't this much suffering for this much sinning. The Atonement is a different doctrine entirely. This is what Paul was so upset about when the Jews tried to preach that doctrine. We've got that back in our Church being taught like that today.

What does Amulec say the key to the Atonement was? He explained that it was Jesus going on that cross. It had to be somebody—not you or me—but someone who is "infinitely loved."

That means "universally" loved, or infinitely loved.

This personally would be such a terrible torture for him in his role as our leader, that the sense of compassion in every little intelligence would be touched.

It is interesting that you and I feel the same empathy. We are also subject to compassion. Every intelligence the all the creations can be reached. They have a sense of compassion. And it is necessary to somehow reach that sense of compassion sufficient to overcome the demands of justice.

When our Heavenly Father puts us down here, and we try and repent the best we can, we are still unworthy to come back to him. Are we not? It is impossible for us to become totally perfect in this life, don't you agree to that? "All have sinned and come short of the glory of God." Doesn't that sound familiar?

We can't become perfect in this life and don't qualify to automatically return to the Father. Those little intelligences would say, "Father, remember you held us back. You can't overlook them."

Our Father wanted us to come here and learn the difference between good and evil—making mistakes and learning from them as we go. But then it becomes impossible for Him to bring us back into His presence. Do you see the problem? So how does he get us back?

First, he asks us to do the very best we can. And then he explains how it has been worked out. He has found out how we can reach the compassion of those little intelligences and overcome the demands of justice without loosing His power or honor.

So when Jesus is on that cross, that suffering has got to be so terrible, that it is infinite in its persuasive power. And because we mean so much to him, that when he pleads for us, he doesn't do it because of our righteousness alone—because it wasn't that good. We did the best we could but it still wasn't perfect.

Jesus then pleads, "They have done the best they could. Now, for my sake, will you let them come up? Otherwise I will be robbed of my reward of my labor. Will you let them come up?"

The reply is, "Jehovah, not for their sake because they were imperfect. But if they mean that much to you, let them come up."

Amulec explains that the compassion that has been created in those little intelligences is enough to overcome the demands of justice. This is in Alma 34:15-16.

The Atonement is not based on the law of "so much suffering for so much sin." It is based on mercy and love. That's all it is based on. It is those little intelligences saying, "Alright, Jehovah, if they mean that much to you after all the suffering you went through, let them come up.

Now how much did Jesus suffer?

When Jesus was dedicated as the eldest son in the Temple, an old man came hurrying up to them His name was Simian. The Holy Ghost had whispered to him, "Rush to the Temple today, you will see the face of the Messiah. And as I promised you before, you will not die until you have seen him."

So he came up to the little group, took that tiny baby out of the arms of Mary and said, "Now oh Lord God Jehovah, let me depart in peace; for mine eyes have beheld thy salvation, the glory of thy people Israel and the light unto the Gentiles."

Then he handed the baby back and said, "Because of him, little mother, one day will pierce your soul like a sword."

Thirty-three years later, on Golgotha—the place of the skull— she witnessed that beloved boy of hers nailed to that cross; spiked with a crown of thorns on his head; blood on his face, lacerated, sweating, and crying out in pain and suffering. What do you think that did to that mother?

It was so intense, that the Father had to do one final thing to make this event supreme. He had to withdraw his spirit from Jesus.

That spirit had sustained Jesus as it sustains all of us up to a point, because it is in all of us. So all of the sudden, the Father withdrew his spirit from Jesus.

As it left him, Jesus cried out, "Eloi, Eloi, lama sabaksani" which translated means, "My God, my God. Why hast thou forsaken me?"

Then, the spirit came back, and Jesus said, I did it! It is finished. "Father, into thy hands I commend my spirit." And he died.

At that moment, Jesus became the Christ.

I gradually came to understand the significance of this event, and realized the suffering of the Father, which was a terrible experience for Him. When he had to tell his son in the Garden of Gethsemane that it was absolutely necessary for Jesus to go through with this suffering, and then when he had to withdraw his spirit from him on the cross—that was a terrible experience for the Father.

The Book of Mormon tells us that the reason Abraham was commanded to slay his own son, Isaac, was so that one earthly father would at least know what it was like to have the roll of the Father, and have to sacrifice your son.

Abraham didn't have to go through with the sacrifice, but he was reconciled to it. He was proceeding to complete the sacrifice because he knew it was for a righteous purpose he didn't understand.

So the Father wanted at least one man to know a little what its like to be subjected to this terrible circumstance of having his son sacrificed under his own hand, and be the Father.

On that day on Golgotha, Jesus became the Christ.

Eventually this event began to clarify in my mind and I began to see what the meaning was of Jesus on that cross. He has become my personal Savior.

I love Jesus.

I love my Heavenly Father.

Never before had I realized what they went through for me, my children and for you all the rest of us. I have learned to love the Father and his Son with all my heart, and feel closer to them.

I love to testify about them. I love to testify of their great mission to us, and their great sacrifice—both the Father and the Son and what they went through for our sakes.

Quite often I am asked down here in Texas where I speak quite often, "Dr. Skousen, are you saved?"

Usually I reply by saying, "Thank you for asking me that. May I bear you my witness?" They are used that. They want to hear my "witness."

And I might say to them:

"I have accepted Jesus Christ as my personal Savior. I have asked my Heavenly Father to forgive my sins. I have made a commitment to my Heavenly Father that I will obey all his commandments by going down into the waters of baptism by immersion and being ministered to by one having authority.

"Then I have had hands laid upon my head by one holding

the Holy Mechizedek Priesthood so that I could receive the great Gift of the Holy Ghost.

"Now I am endeavoring to endure to the end, that I might have the great privilege of overcoming the very last hurdle—death; and being resurrected to glory and going back unto the Father.

"That is my witness."

These wonderful Baptists will put their arms around you and say,

"Thank you, brother, for your testimony."

I appeared here on radio and television about three weeks ago. The minister who interviewed me, and a group of them will be interviewing me this afternoon, they asked me to join them in their prayer room.

So I did. We all took hold of hands. One of the ministers bowed his head and asked that the work we were doing be blessed and that we would each be blessed in or desire to serve God.

The spirit of the Lord was in that circle. The spirit of brotherhood was there. We were all children out of the preexistence, standing there together. They were all Baptists, and I was a Mormon. But we were praying to the same Heavenly Father.

Recently I was invited by the largest Methodist church in Tulsa, Oklahoma and the largest Baptist church in Tulsa, to teach all their people and their friends the wonderful success formula that God inspired the Founding Fathers to write down as our Constitution.

God said it was inspired. In fact he said if its "anything more or less than this, it is evil."

This course on the Constitution is about thirteen hours of instruction. 1250 people sat in that lovely auditorium at the Oral Roberts University.

While I was giving this seminar, during a rest period, the Methodist minister came up to me and said, "Dr. Skousen, what Church do you belong to?"

I thought just to kind of keep the conversation going, I said, "Well what Church would you think I belong to?" I thought he would say that since I was from Salt Lake City, I supposed you would be a Mormon. But he didn't say that.

He said, "Well, of course I'm a Methodist. You sound like a Methodist to me."

And I said, "Well, let's just say I am a committed Christian."

He answered, "I could tell that from your talk."

Then somebody came up and interrupted us and I didn't ever get to tell him what Church I belonged to. That bothered me and I really wanted to tell him before I left.

As we were just concluding the seminars, this ministered came back up to me and said, "Dr. Skousen, I understand you are a Mormon."

And I said, "Yes."

He said, "There must be different kinds of Mormons."

I said, "Well, I guess there are. There are different kinds of all denominations, but I just try to be a standard, run-of-the-mill Mormon. I'm just a traditional Mormon."

He said, "You don't fit the literature I have in the front of my church."

I said, "Well it was probably written by somebody who doesn't really understand the Mormon people."

He asked me, "You do believe in Christ, don't you?"

I said, "Oh yes, that's our real name, 'The Church of Jesus Christ' and the saints are the members of the latter-days. And all they try to do is share the message that the Gospel's been restored and we're preparing for the Second Coming. That's what John Wesley said to look for. To live a methodical Christian life and study the scriptures methodically so all the people would recognize the restoration when it came."

"So that's what you're preaching? It's already in process?"

"Yes, we're preparing for the Second Coming and inviting everyone to come and join us."

He said, "Well, what a beautiful message."

I said, "It is a beautiful message and some great things are going to happen."

He just put his arm around my shoulder and said, "God bless you, brother. God bless you" and walked away.

You missionaries are in a very rich field, where the descendants of father Abraham dwell in abundance. If you will let the spirit work on them, bare your testimony to them and take advantage of these wonderful resources the Brethren have provided.

Be valiant in your calling, from morning until night. Be a good student. Mark your books; study it out; be prayerful; try to understand God's science of salvation. That's all I've been talking about this morning: The real science of salvation and why the atonement was necessary—and it was!

We've talked about why the Father couldn't save us and why he said his Son is the only name given under heaven whereby we may be saved; so that we will realize they have done their part. Now we've got to do is ours. That's why Jesus makes such a plea to us.

In closing, let's turn to D&C 19:15

"Therefore I command you to repent. Repent lest I smite you by the rod of my mouth."

You see he is a god of love but he also has to be a god of justice, or the intelligences would loose confidence in him.

"And by my anger and your suffering be sore, how sore you know not, how exquisite you know not. Ye, how hard to bear you know not. For behold I God have suffered the things for all that they might not suffer if the repent."

In other words, what we do is to repent in order to qualify.

"But if they would not repent, they must suffer even as I."

Now notice how terrible it was:

"Which suffering caused my self even God, the greatest of all, to tremble because of pain; and to bleed at every pore; and to suffer both body and spirit; and would that I might not drink the bitter cup and shrink."

Then verse 19 is wonderful:

"Nevertheless, I partook and finished my preparation unto the children of men."

It is like he is saying to us "I did it! I did it! I was so frightened. I was so scared. I trembled. I ask the Father not to make me go through with it. He said I didn't have to, but he let me know the consequences with no doubt. And I did it!"

He's just so thrilled about it! Then he says not to let that effort be wasted.

Turn now to D&C 45:3.

"Listen to him who is the advocate with the Father; who is pleading your cause before him."

The Father loves us as much as the son. It actually is His plan anyway. This is what Jesus stated in the preexistence: Father, I will do it the way you want it done. Lucifer wanted it done a different way and demanded to take the credit. But the Son said he would do it just as it had been done before. He would do it and accept the pain and suffering.

Let us continue:

"Behold the suffering and death of him who did no sin; in whom thou wast well pleased. Behold the blood of they son which was shed. The blood of him whom thou gavest that thy self might be glorified."

"Wherefore Father, spare these thy brethren that believe on my name that they may come unto me and have everlasting life."

Now turn to Alma 34:14 and we have our concluding thought from Amulek—a great tribute to the Savior and what his sacrifice accomplished:

"And behold this is whole meaning of the law [meaning the law of Moses]. Every whit pointing to that great last sacrifice; and that great and last sacrifice will be the son of God, ye, infinite and eternal [it's going to reach every corner of the universe]."

"And thus he shall bring salvation to all those who shall believe on his name. This being the intent of this last sacrifice; to bring about the bowels of mercy which overpower justice. And bringeth about the means unto men that they may have faith unto repentance.

"And thus mercy can satisfy the demands of justice and encircle them in the arms of safety. While he who exercises not faith unto repentance is exposed to the whole law of the demands of justice."

Now, this is what you Elders and Sisters are in the mission field to tell about.

The story that I've told you this morning, the one that we worked out with such difficulty, is the most profound principle of the Gospel—the Atonement, and why it is necessary.

So that isn't what you preach as missionaries. But that is what you must know in order to preach and testify of Christ.

Let me now give you an example, as we finish, of Abraham Lincoln. I just want to show you how this happens every day in real life. If you want to see how mercy overcomes the demands of justice, watch this:

There was a boy fighting in the Union forces, 19 years old. He went to sleep on guard duty. The opposition broke through and wiped out a whole flank of the army, several hundred were killed, including some of the best friends of this young man.

But he survived.

He was court-martialed and sentenced to die. He expected to die. He thought it was only just that he should die.

President Lincoln was about ready to sign his death warrant for his execution, when a little mother appears on the scene.

She said to him, "President Lincoln, when this war started I had a husband and six sons. First I lost my husband, and one by one I lost five of my sons. Now I only have one son left, and he is sentenced to be executed by a firing squad because he went to sleep on duty.

"He feels awfully bad. He lost some of his best friends and he expects to die.

"President Lincoln. I'm not asking you to spare his life for his sake, but for his mother's sake. He's all I have left. For my sake, could you spare him?"

President Lincoln said, "For your sake, little mother, I will spare him."

As far as I know, President Lincoln was never criticized for that decision.

Does that touch the heart of compassion? Notice how that overcame the demands of justice: "For her sake, I will spare him."

That is what has happened for us. The salvation of Jesus Christ is very real. The price he paid is very terrible.

You are here to testify that Jesus is the Christ and that the

Gospel has been restored to prepare for his Second Coming.

Now that is our mission.

I went into the mission field thinking that testifying of the restoration was my whole mission. No! That is incidental. The divinity if Jesus Christ is our main message.

The fact that he has now spoken to Prophets and raised them up and they are walking the earth—the Priesthood is back!

That is our Good News. We're preparing for the second Christmas when there will be a thousand years of peace on earth good will toward men. I only pray that God will bless every one of us to fulfill our callings with valiance; that the Spirit can testify to thousands of his children that Jesus is the Christ.

That is my prayer this beautiful Christmas season in the year 1980. I pray God's richest blessings on you, brothers and sisters, as upon myself.

That our Heavenly Father will not be disappointed in our efforts, and I say it in the name of Jesus Christ, Amen.

The Glory of the Godhead

In one of the most instructive revelations in the entire Doctrine and Covenants the Lord declares:

> *"I give unto you these sayings [this revelation] that you may understand and know how to worship, and know what you worship, that you may come unto the Father in my name and receive of his fullness."* [1]

This tells us three things:

First, there are truths in this revelation that will help us understand the manner in which we should approach the Savior as our Divine Redeemer.

Second, this is impossible unless we know who he really is, and what he represents as we worship him.

Third, it is only as we gain a deeper understanding and appreciation of the origin, history and identity of the Savior that he is able to bring us to his Father where we can receive of his fullness.

As one might expect, this revelation contains many marvelous insights which will receive our careful consideration in the opening portion of this study.

However, before we attempt to apply the elements of this revelation to Jesus Christ, it is essential that we become better acquainted with the Savior's Father. Hebrew scholars often refer to him as "Elohim" or "Eloheim." [2]

Who is Elohim?

Modern revelations, together with some of the newly discovered manuscripts, give us a superb and vastly superior understanding of the identity and supreme majesty of our Heavenly Father. This is precious knowledge which ten thousand Biblical scholars could not have gleaned from all the libraries in the world prior to 1830.

What are some of the highlights from these new sources of information?

First of all, we learn that "Elohim" is not our Heavenly Father's personal name. It is merely a title. It means "Head of the Gods." [3]

This not only clarifies the meaning of "Elohim," but it discloses the fact that there is a plurality of "Gods," and that in the realm where our Father resides, there are many brilliant and intelligent leaders with God-like qualities over whom he presides.

Second, the Father has revealed to his prophets the actual name by which he is known in the heavenly realm from which his divine power emanates to encompass all of his vast kingdoms.

The scripture says:

> *"In the language of Adam, Man of Holiness is his name, and the name of the Only Begotten is the Son of Man, even Jesus Christ."* [4]

This tells us that the personal identification of our Heavenly Father is actually by the name of "Man," and that the identity of Jesus is therefore appropriately designated as "the Son of Man." This also gives us a new and better understanding of this name-word. Man is a person, a very holy person, a divine person. Mankind, therefore, is a generic term referring to those who were begotten of Man. It means that Paul was literally correct when he said: "We are also his offspring." [5]

So "Man" is not referring to gender. Man is the name of a person in whose image all of us were created, both men and women. Had the translators of Genesis truly understood this particular concept they could have said: "So Man created man [as his offspring] in his image, in the image of 'Man' created he him; male and female created he them." [6]

The third surprising thing the Father has revealed about himself is the fact that he was not always God. This revelation is captured in the rather astonishing but well-known statement by prophets of the latter days which says, "As man now is, God once was."

How can this be? For centuries Plato and even Christian philosophers have proclaimed that the God we worship was the Great Beginning of everything, the First Great Cause, who made everything out of nothing. Revelation has disclosed this is what John Taylor called, "philosophical fried froth."

In all the eternities no "thing" was ever made out of nothing. As we shall see in a moment, God has declared that the universe and everything in it was gradually and ingeniously organized out of things that already existed and these things have existed throughout all eternity. In fact, the word "created" in the Bible would have carried a much more accurate signal to the reader if the translators had used the word, "organized." [7]

Furthermore, all this organizing was done by a whole family of supremely intelligent beings who had attained the status of Godhood. Each of them followed a stringent pattern of eternal progression until they were qualified to be assigned a stewardship over a part of the cosmos. Our Heavenly Father achieved the splendor of his present status as the Man of Holiness after aeons of painful progress. He had to go through the most vigorous sweating and straining, learning and testing, just as we are doing on the planet Earth today.

Once the mind-expanding ramifications of these hitherto unknown facts about our Heavenly Father spilled out of the heavens to enlighten the children of Man, a spokesman for the Lord was able to explain it in rather simple terms. For example, the prophet Joseph Smith addressed an audience of around 10,000 people at the General Conference held at Nauvoo, Illinois on April 7, 1844, and said:

> *"God himself was once as we are now, and is an exalted man, and sits enthroned in yonder heavens! That is the great secret. If the veil were rent today, and the great God who holds this world in its orbit, and who upholds all worlds and all things by his power, was to make himself visible ... you would see him like a man in form -- like yourselves in all the person, image, and very form as a man."*

Then he went on to say:

> *"These are incomprehensible ideas to some, but they are simple. It is the first principle of the gospel to know for a certainty the character of God ... and that he was once a man like us; yea, that God himself, the Father of us all, dwelt on an earth, the same as Jesus Christ himself did.... Jesus said, As the Father hath power in himself, even so hath the Son power.... to lay down his body and take it up again.... I do the things I saw my Father do when worlds came rolling into existence. My Father worked out his kingdom with fear and*

trembling, and I must do the same; and when I get my kingdom I shall present it to my Father, so that he may obtain kingdom upon kingdom." [8]

John, the beloved apostle, verifies the fact that Jesus clearly taught his disciples this doctrine. He quotes Jesus as saying:

"The Son can do nothing of himself, but what he seeth the Father do; for what things soever he [the Father] doeth, these also doeth the Son likewise." [9]

Did Elohim have a Father?

If our Heavenly Father had to go through a mortal experience as we are now doing, who was guiding him? Who was giving him commandments and answering his fervent prayers as the Father now answers ours?

On June 16, 1844, only a few weeks after the sermon referred to above, Joseph Smith assured the audience that Elohim did indeed have a father. He said:

"If Jesus Christ was the Son of God and John discovered [the fact] that God, the father of Jesus Christ, had a father, you may suppose that he [God the Father] had a father also. Where was there ever a son without a father.... Paul says that which is earthly is in the likeness of that which is heavenly. Hence, if Jesus had a father, can we not believe that he [God the Father] had a father also?" [10]

Joseph Smith assured his hearers that they could believe these profound principles because "They are given to me by the revelations of Jesus Christ." [11]

Of course if our Heavenly Father was guided through an earthly experience, just as he is presently guiding us, what did he have to do to eventually attain Godhood? Joseph Smith said our Heavenly Father had to do the same thing that all exalted beings have done. He had to "pass beneath all things" just as his Son would later do. This meant the Father had to matriculate from the lowly experiences of mortality up through an escalation of gradual achievement until he attained the highest dimension of celestial exaltation.

Joseph Smith said:

"Here, then, is eternal life -- to know the only wise and true God; and you have got to learn how to be Gods yourselves, and to be kings and priests to God, the same as all the Gods have done before you, namely, by going from one small degree to another, and from a small capacity to a great one; from grace to grace, from exaltation to exaltation, until you attain to the resurrection from the dead ... as do those who sit enthroned in everlasting powers." [12]

The Mission of Jesus Christ

Now that we have gained a deeper insight into the greatness of the Father, and the means by which this glorified "Man of Holiness" attained Godhood, what does Section 93 say about the "Son of Man?"

In this revelation John (apparently John the Baptist[13]) calls the Son of Man the "Word".[14] This has deep significance. It means that during all of the aeons of time when we and other "organized intelligences" were being trained, tested, and assigned our respective places in God's plan, Jesus was the divinely appointed general manager who brought us the "word" from the Father. This is the one to whom we looked for guidance, correction, inspiration, and the one we learned to follow as the perfect example of Godly obedience.

Not only is he the "Word" for us, but he is the "Word" or superintendent for the structural development of all the suns, stars, and planets that were scheduled for our cycle or "round." Five times in the scriptures, the Lord emphasizes that the Father's "course is one eternal round." [15]

In our "round," the Father leaves no doubt that he made Jehovah, or Jesus Christ, exclusively responsible for the organizing, embellishing, and inhabiting of all the "worlds without number" that belong to our particular cycle.

This rather amazing revelation is described in the following scripture:

"And he [Moses] beheld many lands [in verse 33 these lands are called "worlds without number"] *and each land was called [an] earth, and there were inhabitants on the face thereof.*

> *"And it came to pass that Moses called upon God, saying: Tell me, I pray thee, why these things are so, and by what thou madest them?*
>
> *"And behold, the glory of the Lord was upon Moses, so that Moses stood in the presence of God, and talked with him face to face. And the Lord God said unto Moses....*
>
> *"By the word of my power, have I created them, which is mine Only Begotten Son, who is full of grace and truth.*
>
> *"And worlds without number have I created; and I also created them for mine own purpose; and by the Son I created them, which is mine Only Begotten."* [16]

So here we have the Father referring to the "Word" as his "Only Begotten Son," just as he does in D&C 93:8-9.

He not only had the responsibility of organizing all of these millions of planets but superintending the details of providing each one with a beautiful terrain, luxurious foliage, a vast variety of animal life, and eventually peopling each of these "earths" with billions of human beings.

It also appears that all of these fellow human beings who occupy these other "earths" belong to our generation of the Father's children. Therefore they are our spiritual brothers and sisters and are as dependent on the atonement of Jesus Christ for their salvation and exaltation as we are.

It is interesting that when Moses was shown all of those "worlds without number" that belong to Jehovah's stewardship, they were all inhabited simultaneously. This would indicate that they are all part of our "round."

The Father told Moses in a later manifestation that he had created many worlds that had passed away, but these apparently referred to earlier cycles where previous worlds had run their course and passed on to glory. When Moses had originally asked God to show him all of his creations, the Father made an interesting response. He said:

"No man can behold all my works, except he behold
all my glory; and no man can behold all my glory, and
afterwards remain in the flesh on the earth." [17]

So Moses had to be satisfied with the vision of our "round" or cycle.

But even so, what a magnificent vision it must have been! The Psalmist wrote: "The heavens declare the glory of God; and the firmament showeth his handiwork." [18]

No one can gaze into the depthless azure of a starlit night without feeling an awesome sense of splendor and grandeur as we contemplate these countless creations of God's heavenly hosts. Out there, with some of the stars millions of light years away, brilliant luminaries move majestically through the heavens, while solar systems and twinkling constellations of stars synchronize their maneuvers as though they were a vast heavenly clockwork with an intricate assembly of wheels within wheels silently measuring the aeons of eternity.

When Moses saw all of this in vision it made him feel that "man is nothing!"[19] Of course, the Lord eventually got around to explaining that the very essence of God's glory is to "bring to pass the immortality and eternal life of man," [20] so this helped Moses project the importance of mankind back into its proper perspective.

Are We Coming to the End of Our "Round?"

There are several hints that our earth might be the final creation in this cycle, and that when it has run its course the windup scene will take place. Lucifer and his hosts will be eliminated from our system, the earth will be celestialized, others will be set up to accommodate the terrestrial and telestial glories. Furthermore, it is reasonable to suppose that what happens to our earth and our family may be typical of what happens to our spiritual brothers and sisters on their earths.

And because this earth seems to be the final windup scene, it appears that both Jehovah and Lucifer know that the great last battle in the war that began in the pre-mortal existence will be fought on this planet. There is considerable evidence that the inhabitants of this earth have constituted a different mixture of extremely "good" people and extremely "bad" people than have inhabited the other earths shown to Moses. Consider the following:

Since this planet was assigned to be the place where the mortal life, death, and resurrection of the Son of God would take place, we learn that some of Jehovah's closest associates in the pre-mortal existence were reserved to be the patriarchs, prophets, apostles, and leaders of his Church here on this earth. In other words, to a considerable extent, this earth was assigned some of the very best of the Father's children.

In contrast to this, the scripture is very clear that this earth has also been inhabited by some of the very worst of all God's children.

Consider, for example, the Lord's revelation to Enoch concerning the total debauchery and degradation that would exist in Noah's day. As the vision unfolded, Enoch saw the Lord weeping:

> *"And Enoch said unto the Lord: How is it that thou canst weep, seeing thou art holy, and from all eternity to all eternity?....*
>
> *"The Lord said unto Enoch: Behold these thy brethren; they are the workmanship of mine own hands, and I gave unto them their knowledge, in the day I created them; and in the Garden of Eden, gave I unto man his agency;*
>
> *"And unto thy brethren have I said.... that they should love one another, and that they should choose me, their Father; but behold, they are without affection, and they hate their own blood.... among all the work-manship of mine hands there has not been so great wickedness as among thy brethren."* [21]

This would suggest that on all of the other planets which belong to our "round," life has been much more congenial than ours. It would further suggest that they might have never experienced the necessity of a universal flood such as the grossly depraved wicked in the days of Noah suffered on this earth.

A further reference to the concentration of exceptionally wicked spirits on this earth is found in the following scripture:

> *"It must needs be expedient that Christ ... should come among ... those who are the more wicked part of the world; and they shall crucify him -- for thus it*

behooveth our God, and there is none other nation on earth that would crucify their God.

"For should the mighty miracles be wrought among other nations they would repent, and know that he be their God.

"But because of priestcrafts and iniquities, they at Jerusalem will stiffen their necks against him, that he be crucified." [22]

This scripture would lead us to conclude that none of these other worlds, or even the various marvelous demonstration of miraculous power that he poured out upon his own people.

A final observation is that since the inhabitants of this earth have included the worst as well as the best of humanity, it might account for the continuous conflict and widespread orgy of bloodshed and war that have characterized the violent history of our planet. It has indeed been so ferocious, ugly, and revolting that many have wondered how a loving God could even permit it. Only when we have the benefit of modern revelation do we begin to grasp the dimensions of the amazing and sometimes tragic drama that is being played out on this planet.

How Jehovah was Prepared for His Great Mission

Section 93 of the Doctrine and Covenants has a most enlightening passage concerning the preparation of Jehovah for his great mission. Since this had prev-iously been revealed to John the Baptist, [23] the Lord let him tell the story.

We learn that John was allowed to see the history of Jesus Christ from the very "beginning." However, we cannot help but ask, "The beginning of what?" It appears that it was the beginning of our own "round" or cycle.

The first step was to select from among the masses of intelligences the one who was the most outstanding so that he could be trained to be the organizer and manager of this entire "round."

Of all the intelligences that the Father had been training and testing for this particular "round," Jesus was the most brilliant, the most valiant, the most loyal, and the most obedient.

Therefore, as was pointed out by the Christian historian, Eusebius, who lived in the fourth century, Jesus was begotten of the Father as his Firstborn in the spirit world. Eusebius states that the text of the 110th Psalm, 4th verse, originally referred to the time when Jesus was born of a heavenly mother. He quotes it as saying "Out of the womb, before the morning star have I begotten thee." [24]

Paul points out that Jesus was not only the Firstborn "among many brethren" [25] but he was born first so that he could be in charge of all the subsequent creations during this "round."

Paul said Jesus is in:

"... the image of the invisible God, the firstborn of every creature:

"For by him were all things created, that are in heaven, and that are in earth, visible and invisible, whether they be thrones, or dominions, or principalities, or powers: all things were created by him, and for him:

"And he is before all things, and by him all things consist." [26]

In a modern revelation, Jesus adds his own testimony by saying:

"And now, verily I say unto you, I was in the beginning with the Father, and am the Firstborn;

"And all those who are begotten through me are partakers of the glory of the same, and are the church of the firstborn." [27]

In the Spirit World Jesus Had to Grow from Grace to Grace

Section 93 of the Doctrine and Covenants has another diadem of important truth which was new to modern gospel scholars. John emphasized that in the beginning Jesus was not fully prepared for his place in the Godhead. He had to be carefully tutored and trained before he could become the Father's superintendent and production manager for our round.

Here is what this scripture says:

> *"And I, John, saw that he received not of the fullness*
> *at the first, but received grace for grace;*
>
> *"And he received not of the fullness at first, but*
> *continued from grace to grace, until he received a*
> *fullness;*
>
> *"And thus he was called the Son of God, because he*
> *received not of the fullness at the first."* [28]

The "fullness" apparently refers to a "fullness of truth," because this scripture says that as he grew from grace to grace, he finally reached a point where "He received a fullness of truth ... and knoweth all things." [29]

And then this scripture defines truth as:

> *"knowledge of things as they are, and as they were, and*
> *as they are to come."* [30]

This would mean that after graduating from his training course, Jesus knew everything in the past, everything that exists at any given moment of the present, and he learned what would transpire in the future.

Thus, having attained this stupendous pinnacle of supreme intelligence, knowledge, and training, Jesus assumed the role of God's sovereign prime minister in the eternal galactical dimensions of the Father's vast dominions programmed for our cycle or round.

Questions for Reflection and Discussion

1. By the time the gospel was restored both the Jews and the Christians had completely lost the concept of the "family of the Gods." Have you any idea how this could have happened?

2. Does the revelation that the name of our Heavenly Father is "Man of Holiness" have any special meaning or significance to you? How would you explain this to a non-member friend?

3. On April 7, 1844, which was just a short time before the death of Joseph Smith, he announced that as we are now, God once was, and as God now is, we may become. If you had been an early convert to the Church at that time do you think this would have shaken your faith? How do you account for the fact that there was no mass defection from the Church when this amazing new concept was announced at the general conference?

4. Have you previously thought of the Savior as the organizer and superintendent for the setting up of all the millions of planets that belong to our cycle or round?

5. Discuss the Father's disclosure that his course is "one eternal round." What do you think of the suggestion that we may be drawing toward the close of our round?

6. Did it surprise you that Jesus had to grow from grace to grace and get special training in the spirit world before the Father could make him his general manager for this round? Had you thought of that before?

7. Would it appear that Jesus had attained his high office before any of the rest of us or any of the worlds belonging to our round had been given spirit embodiments?

Footnotes

1. D&C 93:19.

2. Hastings Dictionary of the Bible, under "God," vol. II, p. 199.

3. Joseph Smith, Teachings (Salt Lake City, Utah: Deseret Book, 1973), pp. 371-372.

4. Moses 6:57.

5. Acts 17:28.

6. Genesis 1:27.

7. Joseph smith, Teachings (Salt Lake City, Utah: Deseret Book, 1973), p. 350.

8. Joseph Smith, Teachings of the Prophet Joseph Smith (Salt Lake City, Utah: Deseret Book, 1973), p. 345-347.

9. John 5:19.

10. Andrew E. Ehat and Lyndon W. Cook, editors, Words of Joseph Smith, p. 380.

11. The Words of Joseph Smith, p. 346.

12. Joseph Smith, Teachings of Joseph Smith, p. 346-347.

13. See D&C 93:15.

14. D&C 93:8.

15. 1 Nephi 10:19; Alma 7:20; 37:12; D&C 3:2; 35:1.

16. Moses 1:29-33.

17. Moses 1:5.

18. Psalms 19:1.

19. Moses 1:10.

20. Moses 1:39.

21. Moses 7:29-36.

22. 2 Nephi 10:3-5.

23. See D&C 93:15; John 1:34.

24. The Nicene and Post-Nicene Fathers (Grand Rapids: William B. Eerdmans Publishers, 1952), vol. 1, p. 86.

25. Romans 8:29.

26. Colossians 1:15-17.

27. D&C 93:21-22.

28. D&C 93:12-14.

29. D&C 93:26-28.

30. D&C 93:24

Episodes In The Life of
W. Cleon Skousen

Official Autobiography of W. Cleon Skousen

Compiled and edited in his own words by Jo Ann Skousen and Mark Skousen from his extensive journals, letters, interviews and speeches. Includes personal insights, stories, and controversies from a career that spanned more than 70 years.

Hardbound, color, 530 pages

Available at: skousen2000.com and Amazon

Narration available on Audible

Other books and products by W. Cleon Skousen

Treasures from the Book of Mormon Audio Commentary

This audio commentary includes both a complete narration of the Book of Mormon (by Wendell Noble) and a verse-by-verse commentary by Brother Skousen. *Available as a download, USB Flash Drive, or CDs. Also on Audible.*

Church History and Doctrine and Covenants Audio Commentary

D&C narration (Wendell Noble) and verse-by-verse commentary (Cleon Skousen) covering the essential doctrines and early history of the Church. *Available as a download, USB Flash Drive, or CDs. Also on Audible.*

Days of the Living Christ

This popular and insightful book covers and intimate look at the earthly life and mission of the Savior. It covers his premortal assignment to his very last mortal hours on earth. Brother Skousen enlightens and inspires the reader for a meaningful understanding Jesus Christ. *Hardbound, narrations also available*

The Complete Works of W. Cleon Skousen CDrom

This CD actually contains the text of ALL his books and classroom handouts, plus both unpublished works and out-of-print books.

A Gospel Trilogy

This new 2025 Edition covers an extensive insight regarding the role of Elohim, our Heavenly Father, and the Atonement according to revelations received by Joseph Smith. We learn both the MILK and MEAT of the Gospel. *Paperback*